Real-World Machine Learning for Software Leaders

Sachin Medavarapu

Table of Contents

Preface

Machine learning (ML) is rapidly becoming a critical component of modern software engineering. However, most books and courses focus heavily on mathematical theory, often leaving beginners struggling to connect these concepts with practical applications. This book, *Real-World Machine Learning in Software Engineering*, takes a different approach by emphasizing real-world applications to help you understand ML concepts through practical examples.

This book is designed for absolute beginners who have never been exposed to machine learning. It will guide you step by step, explaining key ML algorithms and techniques through real-world use cases. By the end of this book, you will have a solid understanding of machine learning fundamentals, enabling you to dive into intermediate and advanced books with confidence. Moreover, the knowledge gained from this book will help you create an impact in the world of AI/ML by applying ML models effectively in software engineering.

With each chapter, you will learn a different ML concept and how it applies to real-world problems. You will explore various algorithms, including classification techniques, support vector machines, decision trees, ensemble learning, and deep learning architectures such as convolutional neural networks (CNNs) and recurrent neural networks (RNNs). You will also work with unsupervised learning, dimensionality reduction, natural language processing (NLP), and reinforcement learning before finally looking at practical implementations with code.

Let's embark on this journey together and transform theoretical machine learning knowledge into hands-on expertise that can be applied directly to solving real-world challenges in software engineering.

Acknowledgements

I would like to express my deepest gratitude to my beloved family. Your unwavering support, encouragement, and love have been the cornerstone of my journey in the world of machine learning and coding. Your belief in me, even during the most challenging moments, has been a constant source of strength and inspiration. Every step of this journey has been made possible because of your care and understanding, and I dedicate this work to you. Thank you for standing by me and for being my guiding light through every endeavor.

CHAPTER 1

Machine Learning in the Real World

Machine learning has rapidly transitioned from a niche research area to a pivotal technology reshaping numerous industries. As we embark on this exploration of machine learning's transformative power, it becomes essential to understand both its theoretical underpinnings and practical applications. In this chapter, we introduce the fundamental concepts of machine learning, including supervised and unsupervised learning, examine the challenges faced when applying these methods in real-world scenarios, and discuss how diverse industries such as finance, healthcare, and automation are leveraging these advancements.

Introduction: The Emergence of Machine Learning

Over the past few decades, machine learning has grown from experimental algorithms into robust systems that can predict trends, automate decision-making, and solve complex problems. This evolution is driven by increased computational power, vast amounts of data, and significant advances in algorithmic design. Today, organizations rely on machine learning to enhance customer experiences, optimize operations, and even save lives.

Machine learning is not merely about building predictive models. It is about understanding patterns hidden within data, automating routine tasks, and providing insights that were previously unattainable. In this context, the real-world impact of machine learning is profound. For instance, in finance, algorithms detect fraudulent transactions in real time. In healthcare, machine learning aids in diagnosing diseases with high accuracy. In automation, it enhances the efficiency of manufacturing processes.

The goal of this chapter is to bridge the gap between abstract theoretical models and their practical implementations. We will explore the basic building blocks of machine learning, delve into specific learning paradigms, and highlight the challenges and triumphs of applying these techniques in dynamic, real-world environments.

Understanding Machine Learning Fundamentals

Defining Machine Learning

At its core, machine learning is a subset of artificial intelligence that involves the creation of algorithms capable of learning from data. Unlike traditional programming, where instructions are explicitly coded, machine learning models are designed to improve their performance as they are exposed to more data over time. This adaptive capability allows

1

systems to handle tasks such as prediction, classification, and decision-making without needing constant human oversight.

The Learning Process

The typical machine learning process involves several key steps:

1. Data Collection and Preparation: Data is the lifeblood of machine learning. The process begins with gathering relevant datasets, cleaning the data, and transforming it into a format suitable for analysis.

2. Feature Selection and Extraction: Not all data points are equally useful. Identifying which features (variables) contribute most significantly to the predictive power of the model is crucial.

3. Model Selection: Depending on the nature of the problem, different types of algorithms, ranging from linear regression models to complex neural networks, can be employed.

4. Training and Validation: The selected model is trained on a portion of the data and then validated using another segment to ensure its accuracy and robustness.

5. Testing and Deployment: Once validated, the model is tested on unseen data to assess its performance in real-world conditions before being deployed in production environments.

Key Learning Paradigms

Supervised Learning: Teaching by Example

Supervised learning is perhaps the most well-known paradigm in machine learning. In this approach, models are trained on labeled datasets, where the correct output is provided for each example in the training set. The objective is for the model to learn a mapping from inputs to outputs so that it can accurately predict the outcome for new, unseen data.

How Supervised Learning Works

In supervised learning, the dataset is divided into two main parts: the training set and the test set. During the training phase, the algorithm learns from the examples provided, adjusting its parameters to minimize the error between its predictions and the actual outputs. Once the model has been adequately trained, it is evaluated on the test set to measure its predictive performance.

Common Algorithms

Several algorithms are widely used in supervised learning, including:

- Linear Regression: Used for predicting continuous values, linear regression establishes a linear relationship between input features and the target variable.

- Logistic Regression: Despite its name, logistic regression is used for binary classification tasks. It estimates the probability that an input belongs to a certain class.

- Decision Trees and Random Forests: These are popular for both classification and regression. Decision trees break down data into smaller subsets, while random forests improve accuracy by averaging multiple decision trees.

- Support Vector Machines (SVMs): SVMs are effective for high-dimensional spaces and are often used for classification problems.

- Neural Networks: Inspired by the human brain, neural networks can model complex non-linear relationships and are the foundation of deep learning.

Applications in the Real World

Supervised learning techniques are used extensively across industries. For example:

- Finance: Algorithms detect fraudulent activities by learning from historical transaction data.

- Healthcare: Diagnostic tools utilize supervised learning to classify medical images, aiding in early disease detection.

- Retail: Recommendation systems leverage customer purchase history to suggest new products.

The success of supervised learning hinges on the availability of high-quality, labeled data. When such data is abundant, these models can achieve impressive levels of accuracy and reliability.

Unsupervised Learning: Discovering Hidden Patterns

Unlike supervised learning, unsupervised learning does not rely on labeled datasets. Instead, the algorithm is tasked with finding structure and patterns within the data on its own. This approach is particularly useful when the underlying structure of the data is unknown or when labeling is prohibitively expensive.

Core Techniques

Unsupervised learning encompasses a variety of techniques, with clustering and dimensionality reduction being the most prominent.

- Clustering: This technique groups similar data points together. Algorithms like k-means and hierarchical clustering are common examples. Clustering is invaluable for market segmentation, where customers are grouped based on purchasing behavior, and for anomaly detection, where outliers are identified.

- Dimensionality Reduction: High-dimensional data can be challenging to analyze. Dimensionality reduction techniques, such as Principal Component Analysis (PCA) and t-Distributed Stochastic Neighbor Embedding (t-SNE), simplify data by reducing the number of features while preserving its intrinsic structure. This not only makes the data easier to visualize but also improves the efficiency of subsequent analyses.

Real-World Challenges in Machine Learning

While the theoretical promise of machine learning is immense, real-world applications come with a host of challenges. These obstacles must be navigated to harness the true potential of machine learning in practice.

- Data Quality and Availability: Real-world data is often noisy, incomplete, or biased. Poor data quality can lead to models that underperform or, worse, perpetuate existing biases.

- Scalability and Computation: As datasets grow larger, the computational demands of training machine learning models increase dramatically.

- Interpretability and Transparency: In many domains, it is essential that machine learning models provide interpretable and transparent results.

- Ethical and Privacy Concerns: Issues such as data privacy and algorithmic bias require responsible AI governance.

Industry Adoption: Transforming Sectors Across the Board

The impact of machine learning is perhaps best illustrated through its diverse applications in industry.

- Finance: Machine learning has revolutionized risk assessment, fraud detection, and algorithmic trading.

- Healthcare: Advanced diagnostic tools powered by machine learning algorithms assist in early detection of diseases.

- Automation and Manufacturing: Machine learning optimizes production lines, predicts maintenance needs, and improves quality control.

Conclusion: The Road Ahead

Machine learning is at the forefront of a technological revolution that is redefining the way data is utilized to solve real-world problems. This chapter has provided a comprehensive overview of key concepts, from supervised and unsupervised learning to challenges and ethical considerations.

As machine learning continues to evolve, its integration into everyday life will expand. The lessons learned from current applications will pave the way for future innovations, ensuring that machine learning remains a driving force behind technological progress.

In the chapters that follow, deeper explorations of specific algorithms, advanced topics like deep learning, and real-world case studies will highlight the full spectrum of machine learning's capabilities. The journey of understanding and applying machine learning is one of continual learning and adaptation, where every challenge presents an opportunity to innovate and improve.

CHAPTER 2

Classification in Real World

Classification is one of the most fundamental techniques in machine learning for categorizing data into distinct classes. This chapter provides an in-depth look at various classification methods, including logistic regression, decision trees, support vector machines (SVMs), and neural networks. We will discuss the mathematical foundations and algorithmic structures of these techniques and illustrate their application in real-world domains such as spam filtering, medical diagnosis, and fraud detection. By understanding the strengths and limitations of each approach, practitioners can make informed decisions when selecting models for specific tasks.

Introduction to Classification

Classification involves assigning input data into one of several predefined categories. In many scenarios, decisions need to be made rapidly and accurately based on incoming data. For example, a system may need to decide whether an email is spam or not, determine if a patient is suffering from a particular disease, or flag a financial transaction as fraudulent. Classification techniques enable systems to make these decisions automatically by learning patterns from historical data.

The process of classification typically involves two phases: training and testing. During the training phase, a classifier learns to map input features to their corresponding labels by analyzing a labeled dataset. Once the classifier is trained, it is tested on new data to assess its performance. The accuracy, precision, recall, and other metrics are used to evaluate how well the classifier generalizes to unseen data. This evaluation process is crucial because a model that performs well on training data might not necessarily work well in a real-world environment.

Another critical aspect of classification is feature engineering. The quality and relevance of the input features have a significant impact on the classifier's performance. Features must capture the essence of the data and be representative of the underlying patterns that distinguish one class from another. In some cases, feature selection and dimensionality reduction techniques are employed to enhance model performance and reduce computational complexity.

Logistic Regression

Logistic regression is one of the simplest and most widely used classification techniques. Despite its name, logistic regression is used for classification tasks rather than regression. The algorithm models the probability that a given input belongs to a particular class. It uses a logistic function, also known as the sigmoid function, to squeeze the output of a linear equation into a range between 0 and 1. This probability is then used to classify the input.

The mathematical foundation of logistic regression is based on the logistic function:

$$P(y=1|X) = \frac{1}{1 + e^{-z}}$$

where z is a linear combination of the input features and their corresponding weights. The model is trained by adjusting these weights to minimize the difference between the predicted probabilities and the actual outcomes using a cost function, typically the cross-entropy loss.

One of the strengths of logistic regression is its interpretability. The coefficients obtained from the model provide insights into how each feature influences the probability of a given outcome. This feature makes logistic regression especially useful in applications such as medical diagnosis, where understanding the impact of various factors on disease prediction is critical.

In practice, logistic regression has been successfully applied in domains such as spam filtering. By analyzing features like word frequency and email metadata, logistic regression models can efficiently classify emails as spam or not spam. Additionally, in medical diagnosis, logistic regression assists in predicting the presence or absence of a condition based on clinical variables.

Decision Trees

Decision trees are a non-parametric method used for both classification and regression. A decision tree recursively splits the input space into regions based on feature values. Each internal node represents a decision based on a feature, and each branch corresponds to an outcome of that decision. The leaves of the tree represent the final classification outcomes.

The process of building a decision tree involves selecting the feature that best separates the data into distinct classes. Metrics such as information gain, Gini impurity, or entropy are often used to decide the optimal splits. The recursive partitioning continues until a stopping criterion is met, such as a minimum number of samples in a node or a maximum tree depth.

One of the key advantages of decision trees is their ease of interpretation. The tree structure visually represents the decision-making process, allowing stakeholders to trace the reasoning behind each classification decision. This transparency is particularly beneficial in fields where explainability is crucial, such as fraud detection and medical diagnosis.

Decision trees have also been extended into ensemble methods, such as random forests and gradient boosting machines. These ensemble techniques combine the predictions of multiple trees to improve accuracy and robustness. In fraud detection, ensemble methods are frequently used to analyze transaction patterns and identify anomalous behavior that might indicate fraudulent activity.

Support Vector Machines

Support vector machines (SVMs) are powerful classifiers that work well in high-dimensional spaces. The core idea behind SVMs is to find a hyperplane that best separates the classes in the feature space. For a binary classification problem, the SVM algorithm seeks the hyperplane that maximizes the margin between the two classes. This margin is defined as the distance between the hyperplane and the nearest data points from each class, which are known as support vectors.

Mathematically, the optimization problem solved by an SVM involves minimizing the norm of the weight vector subject to constraints that ensure correct classification of the training data. In cases where the data is not linearly separable, kernel functions are used to transform the input space into a higher-dimensional space where a separating hyperplane can be found. Common kernels include the linear kernel, polynomial kernel, and radial basis function (RBF) kernel.

SVMs are particularly effective in situations where the number of dimensions is large relative to the number of samples. Their robustness to overfitting, especially when using regularization parameters, makes them suitable for various applications. In spam filtering, SVMs have been employed to classify emails based on content and metadata. The ability to handle complex, non-linear boundaries also makes SVMs attractive for tasks in medical diagnosis, where subtle differences in patient data may separate different conditions.

Despite their advantages, SVMs require careful tuning of parameters and can be computationally intensive for very large datasets. Nonetheless, their performance in high-dimensional classification problems continues to make them a popular choice among researchers and practitioners.

Neural Networks

Neural networks are a class of models inspired by the human brain that have gained popularity due to their ability to model complex, non-linear relationships. At their simplest, neural networks consist of layers of interconnected nodes, or neurons, each performing a weighted sum of inputs followed by a non-linear activation function. The simplest form is the feedforward neural network, where information flows in one direction from the input layer to the output layer.

The training of neural networks involves adjusting the weights of the connections using an algorithm called backpropagation. This method calculates the gradient of the loss function with respect to each weight and updates the weights to minimize the error. Neural networks are highly flexible and can be designed with multiple hidden layers to capture intricate patterns in the data. When deep architectures are used, the models are referred to as deep neural networks.

One of the greatest strengths of neural networks is their versatility. They have been successfully applied to a wide range of classification tasks, including image recognition, natural language processing, and time-series analysis. In the context of spam filtering, neural networks can learn to recognize complex patterns in text and metadata that indicate spam. Similarly, in medical diagnosis, neural networks can analyze imaging data and electronic health records to predict the presence of diseases with high accuracy.

The flexibility of neural networks also comes with challenges. They require large amounts of data and significant computational resources to train effectively. Additionally, the resulting models are often seen as "black boxes" because their decision-making process is not easily interpretable. Despite these challenges, advancements in techniques for model interpretation and the development of specialized hardware have made neural networks one of the most powerful tools in the classification toolbox.

Applications in the Real World

Classification techniques have found widespread application in numerous real-world scenarios. In this section, we highlight three prominent applications: spam filtering, medical diagnosis, and fraud detection.

Spam Filtering

Spam filtering is one of the earliest and most practical applications of classification in machine learning. The goal is to automatically detect and filter out unwanted email messages from the inbox. Various classification algorithms, including logistic regression, SVMs, and neural networks, have been employed to distinguish spam emails from legitimate ones. Features such as word frequency, sender information, and the presence of specific keywords are used to train the models. High accuracy in spam detection not only improves user experience but also enhances cybersecurity by reducing the risk of phishing attacks.

Medical Diagnosis

In the medical field, classification algorithms are used to aid in the diagnosis of diseases. Machine learning models can analyze patient data, including symptoms, test results, and imaging studies, to predict the likelihood of a particular condition. Logistic regression provides insights into the influence of specific clinical features, while neural networks can capture complex interactions between variables. Accurate classification in medical diagnosis can lead to earlier intervention and improved patient outcomes. However, the use of machine learning in healthcare also necessitates a high degree of interpretability and trust, as decisions have significant consequences for patient health.

Fraud Detection

Fraud detection in the financial industry is a critical application of classification techniques. Fraudulent activities, such as unauthorized transactions and identity theft, must be identified in real time to prevent financial losses. Decision trees and ensemble methods are commonly used to analyze transaction patterns and flag anomalies that might indicate fraudulent behavior. SVMs and neural networks further enhance the detection process by modeling complex patterns in the data. The rapid identification and prevention of fraud not only protect customers but also reduce costs for financial institutions.

Challenges and Future Directions

Despite the success of classification techniques in various applications, several challenges remain. Data quality and quantity are critical factors in model performance. In many real-world scenarios, data can be noisy, incomplete, or imbalanced, which affects the accuracy of the classifiers. Techniques such as data augmentation, resampling, and synthetic data generation are often necessary to address these issues.

Another challenge is the interpretability of complex models. While models such as decision trees are inherently transparent, techniques like neural networks require additional methods for explaining their decisions. Researchers are continually developing tools to improve model explainability, which is essential in high-stakes applications such as medical diagnosis and fraud detection.

Scalability also presents a challenge as the volume of data continues to grow exponentially. Developing efficient algorithms that can handle large-scale datasets without compromising performance is an ongoing area of research. Furthermore, the integration of real-time processing capabilities is becoming increasingly important, especially in applications where immediate decisions are critical.

Looking forward, future directions in classification research include the development of hybrid models that combine the strengths of different algorithms. For example, integrating logistic regression with neural network approaches may yield models that are both interpretable and capable of capturing complex patterns. The use of transfer learning, where models pre-trained on one task are adapted to another, is also gaining traction as a way to overcome data scarcity in specific domains.

Conclusion

Classification remains a cornerstone of machine learning with profound implications in the real world. This chapter has explored several key classification techniques, including logistic regression, decision trees, support vector machines, and neural networks. Each method brings its own strengths and challenges, and the choice of algorithm depends on the specific characteristics of the problem at hand.

Through applications in spam filtering, medical diagnosis, and fraud detection, we have seen how classification techniques are deployed to make critical decisions that affect everyday life. As machine learning continues to evolve, advances in algorithm design, data processing, and model interpretability will further enhance the effectiveness of classification systems.

In summary, a deep understanding of classification methods and their practical applications is essential for any practitioner looking to leverage machine learning in the real world. By carefully selecting and tailoring classification models to the unique demands of each application, we can build systems that not only achieve high accuracy but also provide meaningful insights and reliable performance across diverse domains.

CHAPTER 3

Support Vector Machines in the Real World

Support Vector Machines have gained widespread recognition as powerful classifiers in many application areas. In this chapter we explore how Support Vector Machines are used in image recognition, text classification, and bioinformatics. We will explain important concepts such as hyperplanes and kernels in simple language. The aim is to provide a comprehensive overview of how SVMs work in real-world scenarios and to illustrate their practical value through case studies.

Introduction

Support Vector Machines, often abbreviated as SVMs, have become a cornerstone in the world of machine learning. Their ability to handle complex classification tasks has made them a popular choice for researchers and practitioners alike. In fields such as image recognition, text classification, and bioinformatics, SVMs provide robust solutions to problems that require accurate decision-making. This chapter is designed to introduce the key elements of SVMs and to show how they are applied to real-world challenges.

SVMs are based on the idea of finding the best way to separate data into different classes. They accomplish this by identifying a decision boundary that maximizes the separation between classes. By focusing on the most critical data points, SVMs achieve high accuracy even in cases where the differences between classes are subtle. The power of SVMs lies in their flexibility. They are capable of transforming data into higher-dimensional spaces where separation becomes easier. This process is made possible by the use of kernels, which allow the algorithm to work efficiently even with non-linear relationships.

Understanding the Core Concepts of SVMs

The Idea of Separation and Decision Boundaries

The central concept behind Support Vector Machines is the identification of a boundary that separates data into different classes. Imagine a set of points on a piece of paper. Each point belongs to one of two groups. The goal of an SVM is to draw a line that best divides the groups. In higher dimensions the line becomes a flat surface known as a hyperplane.

The quality of a hyperplane is measured by how far it is from the nearest data points in each group. These closest points are called support vectors because they are essential in determining the position of the hyperplane. The greater the distance between the hyperplane and these critical points, the more robust the classification. This means that the SVM is less likely to make mistakes when new data is introduced.

In practical terms the concept of a decision boundary is not just theoretical. When an SVM is deployed in an application such as image recognition the decision boundary may separate images of objects from one another. The SVM learns to distinguish between different visual features and draws the boundary accordingly. The result is a model that is both accurate and reliable even when confronted with new images that were not part of the training set.

The Role of Hyperplanes in Classification

Hyperplanes serve as the decision boundaries in SVMs. In simple terms a hyperplane is a flat surface that divides data points into distinct groups. When working with two-dimensional data the hyperplane is simply a line. As the number of dimensions increases the concept remains the same although the visualization becomes more challenging.

The process of selecting a hyperplane involves finding the one that best separates the classes. The best hyperplane is one that maximizes the gap between the closest points in each class. This gap is referred to as the margin. By maximizing the margin the SVM ensures that the classification model is less sensitive to noise in the data. This approach also helps in reducing the risk of overfitting, where a model might perform well on training data but poorly on new data.

In practice the use of hyperplanes in classification extends beyond simple problems. For example in text classification the features might be words or phrases extracted from documents. The SVM finds the hyperplane that separates documents into categories such as spam and non-spam emails. The flexibility of hyperplanes enables SVMs to handle a wide range of classification tasks across different domains.

The Role of Kernels in SVMs

While the idea of a hyperplane works well for data that is linearly separable, many real-world problems involve data that does not have a clear linear boundary. This is where kernels come into play. Kernels allow SVMs to work in higher-dimensional spaces without the need for complex computations in those spaces.

A kernel is a function that transforms the original data into a new space where the classes become more separable. The transformation is done implicitly, which means that the SVM can perform the classification task without ever explicitly calculating the new coordinates of the data points. This implicit transformation is computationally efficient and makes it possible to handle very complex problems.

There are several types of kernels that can be used depending on the nature of the data. For instance, a linear kernel is suitable for problems where the data can be separated by a straight line or flat hyperplane. In cases where the relationship between features is non-linear a kernel that maps the data into a higher-dimensional space can be used. This flexibility allows SVMs to adapt to a wide variety of problems.

In many practical applications the choice of kernel is critical. For example when classifying images the patterns and textures may not be linearly separable. A non-linear kernel can transform the data so that the SVM is able to identify the underlying structure. Similarly in bioinformatics kernels help in classifying complex biological data, where the relationships between variables are not immediately apparent.

Real-World Applications: Image Recognition

Image recognition is one of the most prominent areas where Support Vector Machines have made a significant impact. In this field the goal is to enable computers to identify objects, scenes, and even specific patterns within images. SVMs are particularly well suited for these tasks because they are capable of handling large amounts of high-dimensional data.

In an image recognition task the first step is to extract meaningful features from the images. These features might include edges, textures, and shapes. Once the features have been extracted the SVM is trained on a dataset where the images have been labeled. The SVM then learns the boundaries that separate different categories of images. For example an SVM may be used to distinguish between images of cats and dogs based on the visual features extracted from the images.

The success of SVMs in image recognition can be attributed to their ability to manage high-dimensional data and to effectively use kernels. Non-linear kernels enable the SVM to capture subtle variations in the images that might be missed by simpler classification techniques. The robustness of the model makes it a reliable choice in environments where accuracy is of utmost importance, such as in security systems and medical imaging.

Moreover, SVMs are often combined with other machine learning techniques to further improve image recognition performance. They serve as a key component in hybrid systems that may use deep learning for feature extraction and SVMs for the final classification stage. This combination leverages the strengths of both approaches, resulting in systems that are both powerful and efficient.

Real-World Applications: Text Classification

Another area where Support Vector Machines excel is text classification. The task of categorizing text documents into topics such as news, reviews, or spam detection requires a classifier that can handle sparse and high-dimensional data. SVMs have been shown to be effective in these tasks due to their ability to find clear separation between classes even when the data is noisy.

Text classification using SVMs typically begins with the conversion of text into numerical features. This process involves techniques such as word counting or more sophisticated methods like term frequency analysis. The resulting feature set is then used to train the SVM. The algorithm learns to distinguish between different text categories by identifying the key words or phrases that are most indicative of each category.

One of the strengths of SVMs in text classification is their robustness in handling irrelevant or redundant features. In a typical text dataset many words may not contribute to the overall meaning of the document. SVMs focus on the most significant features that help in separating the classes, which makes the classification more accurate. This property is particularly useful when dealing with large volumes of text data.

In practical applications SVMs have been deployed in email filtering systems to distinguish between spam and legitimate messages. They are also used in sentiment analysis to determine the mood of a text, whether it is positive, negative, or neutral. The adaptability of SVMs in text classification makes them a valuable tool in various industries such as marketing, finance, and social media analytics.

Real-World Applications: Bioinformatics

Bioinformatics presents a unique set of challenges where the data is often complex and multi-dimensional. Support Vector Machines have found valuable applications in this field, particularly in the classification of biological data. In tasks such as gene expression analysis and protein classification SVMs provide a robust framework for handling the intricacies of biological systems.

The process of classification in bioinformatics involves extracting features from biological data such as DNA sequences or protein structures. The data is then processed and transformed into a format suitable for SVM analysis. The SVM learns to identify patterns and correlations that may not be apparent through traditional analysis methods. This ability to detect subtle patterns makes SVMs an effective tool for predicting biological behavior.

One notable application of SVMs in bioinformatics is in the classification of cancerous versus non-cancerous cells. By analyzing the gene expression profiles, SVMs can help in early detection of cancer and in the development of personalized treatment plans. The accuracy and efficiency of SVMs in this context are critical, as early diagnosis can significantly improve treatment outcomes.

Furthermore SVMs have been employed in protein structure prediction where the task is to classify proteins based on their folding patterns. The complexity of protein structures demands a classification system that can handle non-linear relationships, a need that is effectively met by the use of kernels in SVMs. The use of SVMs in bioinformatics has not only advanced research in the field but also opened up new possibilities in drug discovery and personalized medicine.

Challenges and Future Directions

While Support Vector Machines offer many advantages in real-world applications there remain several challenges that practitioners must address. One challenge is the selection of the appropriate kernel for a given task. The performance of an SVM can vary significantly depending on the choice of kernel and the tuning of its parameters. Finding the optimal configuration often requires extensive experimentation and a deep understanding of the data.

Another challenge lies in the scalability of SVMs when dealing with extremely large datasets. As the volume of data increases the computational resources required to train an SVM may also grow. Researchers are actively working on methods to improve the efficiency of SVM algorithms, such as using approximation techniques and parallel processing methods.

Interpretability is also an area of concern. While SVMs are highly accurate they can be seen as a black box by users who do not have a background in machine learning. Efforts are being made to develop methods that offer more insight into the decision-making process of SVMs so that the models can be trusted in critical applications.

Looking to the future there is a growing interest in hybrid systems that combine the strengths of SVMs with other machine learning techniques. For example many researchers are exploring how SVMs can be integrated with deep learning approaches. In such systems deep learning can be used to extract complex features while SVMs handle the classification task. This synergy promises to push the boundaries of what is possible in applications ranging from autonomous driving to personalized healthcare.

Another area of future research involves the application of SVMs in emerging fields such as Internet of Things and smart cities. With the explosion of sensor data from various devices there is an increasing need for classifiers that can operate in real time. SVMs are well positioned to meet this demand given their efficiency and reliability in processing high-dimensional data.

Conclusion

Support Vector Machines have proven themselves to be versatile and powerful tools in the field of machine learning. Their ability to create clear decision boundaries using hyperplanes and to adapt to non-linear data using kernels has made them indispensable in many applications. In this chapter we have examined the fundamental concepts behind SVMs and explored their applications in image recognition, text classification, and bioinformatics.

The real-world case studies discussed in this chapter illustrate the practical importance of SVMs. In image recognition the robust classification ability of SVMs has led to significant improvements in systems used for security and medical diagnosis. In text classification SVMs have improved the accuracy of email filters and sentiment analysis systems. In bioinformatics SVMs have contributed to advances in early disease detection and protein classification, paving the way for new discoveries in medicine and biology.

While challenges such as kernel selection and scalability remain, ongoing research continues to refine and expand the capabilities of SVMs. The future of Support Vector Machines looks promising as they are integrated with other innovative technologies to address increasingly complex problems. As machine learning continues to evolve the role of SVMs in real-world applications is expected to grow, offering new tools and methods to tackle some of the most pressing challenges in science and industry.

This chapter has provided a detailed overview of how Support Vector Machines work and how they are applied in the real world. By breaking down complex ideas into clear, understandable concepts we hope to have demonstrated both the elegance and the practicality of SVMs. The insights gained here form a foundation for further exploration into the advanced techniques and applications that define the cutting edge of machine learning today.

In summary Support Vector Machines are more than just algorithms; they represent a robust framework that continues to influence the way we solve classification problems in a variety of fields. Their success in practical applications inspires ongoing research and innovation, ensuring that SVMs will remain a vital component of machine learning for years to come.

CHAPTER 4

Decision Trees in the Real World

Decision trees have become one of the most popular and practical machine learning methods for simplifying complex decision-making processes. Their clear structure and ease of interpretation make them especially attractive for applications in fields such as credit risk analysis, customer segmentation, and recommendation systems. In this chapter we explore the inner workings of decision trees, discuss the importance of concepts like tree pruning, entropy, and information gain, and illustrate how these techniques are applied in real world settings.

Introduction to Decision Trees

Decision trees organize information in a hierarchical structure that guides decision making by splitting data into branches based on specific criteria. At each node in the tree the data is divided based on a selected attribute that best distinguishes between different outcomes. This structured approach not only makes it easier for analysts to follow the logic behind the decisions but also helps to automate processes that involve complex criteria.

In the real world decision trees find applications across a variety of industries. For instance banks and financial institutions rely on decision trees to assess credit risk. By evaluating factors such as income levels, credit history, and employment status, decision trees help determine whether a potential customer is likely to repay a loan. Similarly retailers and marketing teams use decision trees for customer segmentation. This involves grouping customers with similar characteristics and behaviors so that marketing strategies can be customized for each segment. In addition online platforms use decision trees to power recommendation systems by learning from past user behavior and suggesting products or services that are most likely to appeal to individual customers.

The intuitive nature of decision trees allows users to quickly grasp how decisions are made and to trace the logic used in each step. As a result decision trees are not only effective analytical tools but also powerful aids in communicating complex ideas to a wide range of audiences.

Fundamental Concepts of Decision Trees

To fully appreciate the power of decision trees it is important to understand some core concepts that underpin their operation. Three key ideas that play a vital role in building robust decision trees are tree pruning, entropy, and information gain.

Tree Pruning

Tree pruning is a process that helps simplify a decision tree by removing branches that do not provide significant insight or that may lead to overfitting. Overfitting occurs when a tree is overly complex and fits the training data too closely, thereby reducing its ability to generalize well to new data. By removing unnecessary branches, pruning creates a more streamlined model that is easier to interpret and more robust when applied to unseen data.

There are different approaches to tree pruning. In some cases the process is carried out during the tree building phase, while in others it is performed after the tree has been fully developed. The goal in each case is to reduce the complexity of the tree while retaining the most valuable predictive elements. This balance is crucial in real world applications where a model that is too complex may be difficult to explain or may react poorly when confronted with data that differs slightly from the training examples.

Entropy

Entropy is a measure of impurity or disorder within a set of data. In the context of decision trees entropy provides a way to evaluate how mixed the data is at any given node. When a node contains examples from a variety of different classes the entropy is high. Conversely when the data is mostly uniform the entropy is low. This concept is important because the objective of constructing a decision tree is to create nodes that are as pure as possible.

In practical terms a high entropy value indicates that the current split does not result in clear decisions and may need further refinement. By continuously measuring entropy as the tree grows the algorithm can decide which splits result in the greatest reduction in disorder. This in turn leads to a tree that more effectively separates the data into clear, well defined groups.

Information Gain

Information gain is the metric used to determine the effectiveness of a particular split in a decision tree. It quantifies the reduction in entropy achieved when a node is divided into branches based on a specific attribute. In essence information gain helps the algorithm decide which attribute is the best candidate to split the data at each stage.

When building a decision tree the algorithm examines the potential splits and selects the one that offers the highest information gain. This choice is crucial because it directs the structure of the tree in a way that maximizes clarity and reduces uncertainty in the decision making process. In practical applications information gain serves as the compass that guides the construction of the tree so that every decision leads to a more precise classification or prediction.

Detailed Discussion on Tree Pruning

Tree pruning is an essential technique that addresses one of the common challenges in machine learning models: overfitting. When a decision tree is allowed to grow without restraint it may start to capture random noise in the training data rather than underlying patterns that hold true in general. This results in a model that performs exceptionally well on training data but falls short when applied to new or unseen data.

Pruning helps by removing parts of the tree that contribute little to the overall predictive power of the model. The process can be thought of as trimming a plant so that it grows in a more balanced and healthy manner. In many real world applications a pruned decision tree is not only easier to understand but also more reliable when making predictions.

There are two common strategies for pruning. The first strategy involves halting the growth of the tree before it becomes overly complex. This proactive approach, sometimes called pre-pruning, sets limits on the depth of the tree or the minimum number of examples required at a node before a split is attempted. The second strategy is post-pruning which allows the tree to be built fully and then simplifies it by removing nodes that do not improve performance on a validation set.

Both approaches have their merits. Pre-pruning can save time during the model building process by reducing the number of computations required. Post-pruning, on the other hand, tends to be more thorough since it considers the full complexity of the tree before making decisions on what to remove. In any case the goal is the same: to develop a model that generalizes well and avoids the pitfalls of being overly tailored to the training data.

In industries such as finance where decisions can have serious consequences the simplicity and reliability provided by pruning is especially valuable. Banks rely on decision trees to assess credit risk and need to ensure that the models used do not give misleading results because of overfitting. Similarly in customer segmentation clear and interpretable trees are preferred since marketing strategies must be based on understandable and transparent rules.

Real World Applications of Decision Trees

The practical impact of decision trees is evident across several industries. In this section we examine how decision trees are applied in credit risk analysis, customer segmentation, and recommendation systems.

Credit Risk Analysis

In the financial industry decision trees are used extensively to evaluate the creditworthiness of potential borrowers. Banks and lending institutions assess numerous factors such as employment history, debt-to-income ratios, and past payment records. A decision tree processes these inputs by breaking them down into a series of simple decisions that lead to a final recommendation. This method is attractive because it produces results that are easily explained to both regulators and customers.

A pruned decision tree in credit risk analysis may have branches that separate applicants based on criteria like stable employment or consistent payment history. By reducing entropy at each split the model isolates the key factors that are most indicative of a borrower's reliability. The information gain associated with each decision ensures that the tree uses the most informative attributes first. The result is a model that can quickly and accurately classify potential borrowers into categories of low, moderate, or high risk.

Customer Segmentation

Customer segmentation is another area where decision trees have found widespread application. In this context the goal is to divide a diverse customer base into distinct groups that share similar behaviors or demographic characteristics. Retailers and service providers use decision trees to analyze customer data and identify patterns that might not be obvious at first glance.

For example a decision tree might split customers based on age, purchase frequency, and product preferences. At each branch the tree uses information gain to select the attribute that best divides the group into more homogeneous subgroups. The process continues until the segments are refined enough to allow for targeted marketing strategies. By understanding the unique traits of each segment the organization can tailor its offerings and communication strategies to match the needs of each group. This leads to higher customer satisfaction and improved sales performance.

Recommendation Systems

Online recommendation systems also benefit from the clarity and structure provided by decision trees. These systems use past user behavior to suggest products, services, or content that might be of interest. A decision tree can analyze various attributes such as browsing history, previous purchases, and user ratings to arrive at a recommendation.

The process starts with splitting the user data based on the most significant preferences. With each branch the system uses entropy and information gain to refine its understanding of what the user likes. The final outcome is a recommendation that is both personalized and relevant. In addition the transparency of decision trees means that recommendations can be explained in simple terms which builds trust with users. They can see the logic behind each suggestion and feel more confident in the choices they make.

Challenges and Best Practices

While decision trees offer many advantages there are also challenges that practitioners must address in real world applications. One challenge is the sensitivity of decision trees to slight changes in the data. Even small variations in the training set can lead to different tree structures which may affect the consistency of predictions. This variability requires careful validation and, in some cases, the use of ensemble methods that combine multiple trees for a more robust outcome.

Another challenge is the tendency for decision trees to become very complex when they try to capture every nuance in the data. This complexity can make the model less interpretable and more difficult to manage. Tree pruning, as discussed earlier, is one way to combat this issue. It is essential for data scientists to strike a balance between model accuracy and interpretability by carefully selecting features and using pruning techniques effectively.

Best practices in using decision trees also involve thorough data preparation. The quality of the data directly impacts the performance of the tree. Data should be cleaned, and missing values handled appropriately before the model is built. In addition it is important to avoid relying on a single decision tree when dealing with highly variable data. Ensemble methods such as random forests may offer additional robustness but come at the cost of reduced interpretability.

In regulated industries such as finance transparency is of utmost importance. Decision trees are often favored because their structure allows analysts to trace the reasoning behind each decision. This transparency aids in meeting regulatory requirements and in building trust with customers who may question the fairness of automated decisions. By following best practices in data handling and model simplification the full potential of decision trees can be realized while minimizing their limitations.

Conclusion

Decision trees stand out as one of the most practical machine learning techniques for addressing complex decision making in the real world. Their inherent clarity and logical structure allow organizations to navigate intricate data landscapes and derive actionable insights with ease. In applications ranging from credit risk analysis to customer segmentation and recommendation systems decision trees help simplify processes and provide transparent outcomes that are easy to interpret.

The concepts of tree pruning, entropy, and information gain are fundamental to the success of decision trees. Pruning ensures that the models remain streamlined and avoid overfitting, while entropy and information gain guide the process of splitting data in a way that minimizes uncertainty. Together these techniques form a robust framework that empowers decision trees to tackle a wide range of challenges in diverse industries.

As technology continues to evolve and data becomes increasingly complex organizations that master decision trees will be well positioned to gain a competitive edge. The ability to explain decisions in clear terms not only improves internal processes but also builds trust with clients and stakeholders. Future developments in machine learning will likely refine these techniques further, making decision trees even more effective as tools for analysis and prediction.

In summary this chapter has explored the use of decision trees in the real world with a focus on their application in credit risk analysis, customer segmentation, and recommendation systems. By understanding and applying the core concepts of tree pruning, entropy, and information gain practitioners can build models that are both accurate and transparent. The insights presented here provide a foundation for further exploration of decision trees and their evolving role in the landscape of modern data analytics.

CHAPTER 5

Ensemble Learning in the Real World

Ensemble learning is a powerful approach that combines multiple models to enhance predictive accuracy and robustness. In many real-world applications, relying on a single model may not capture the full complexity of data. Instead, ensemble methods bring together a variety of learning algorithms to create a more reliable system. This chapter provides an in-depth look at ensemble learning, its core techniques, and its applications in areas such as fraud detection and recommendation systems.

Introduction to Ensemble Learning

Ensemble learning is based on the idea that a collection of diverse models can work together to produce better results than any individual model on its own. The basic intuition is that while each model may have its own biases and errors, these can be minimized when models are combined intelligently. Ensemble methods are not only known for improving accuracy but also for increasing the stability of predictions.

In practical settings, machine learning applications face many challenges. Data can be noisy, incomplete, or highly variable. No single model may capture every nuance in the data. Ensemble learning addresses this issue by integrating different models, each of which may excel in particular situations or on specific subsets of data. The result is a system that is more resilient to fluctuations in data quality and variations in input patterns.

Fundamental Concepts and Benefits

Ensemble learning is built on several key principles. First, diversity among the individual models is essential. Models that make different kinds of errors can complement each other when combined. Second, the method of combination plays a crucial role. Whether models are combined by averaging their outputs or by using more complex stacking techniques, the process must be designed to preserve the strengths of each model.

The benefits of ensemble learning include:

- Improved Accuracy: Combining multiple models tends to cancel out the errors of individual models, leading to a higher overall accuracy.

- Increased Robustness: An ensemble is less sensitive to the shortcomings of any single model. If one model fails, others can compensate.

- Enhanced Generalization: By merging predictions from models trained in different ways, ensemble methods are better able to generalize from training data to unseen data.

- Resilience to Overfitting: When individual models overfit the training data, combining them can reduce the risk of overfitting in the overall ensemble.

Ensemble learning is particularly useful in real-world scenarios where data variability and noise can undermine the performance of a single predictive model.

Techniques in Ensemble Learning

There are several common techniques used in ensemble learning. Each method has its own approach to combining models and is suited to different types of problems.

Bagging

Bagging, or Bootstrap Aggregating, is one of the simplest ensemble techniques. The method involves creating multiple versions of a predictor by generating different training datasets through random sampling with replacement. Each model in the ensemble is trained on a different subset of the data. After training, the predictions of the individual models are combined, usually by taking a majority vote for classification or by averaging for regression.

Bagging reduces the variance of predictions by ensuring that the ensemble is not overly dependent on any single subset of the data. A well-known example of bagging in practice is the Random Forest algorithm, where many decision trees are trained on bootstrapped samples of the data and their outputs are aggregated to produce the final prediction.

Boosting

Boosting is another popular ensemble technique that focuses on training models sequentially. In boosting, each model attempts to correct the errors of its predecessor. The process starts with a base model that is trained on the entire dataset. Subsequent models give more weight to the data points that were misclassified or predicted poorly by earlier models. The final prediction is a weighted combination of all models in the ensemble.

Boosting is particularly effective when models are weak individually but can be made strong by focusing on difficult cases. This technique has led to the development of several well-known algorithms, such as AdaBoost and Gradient Boosting Machines. Boosting is widely used in applications that require high accuracy and the ability to deal with complex data distributions.

Stacking

Stacking, sometimes known as stacked generalization, is a more advanced ensemble technique that combines predictions from several base models using a meta-model. In stacking, multiple individual models are trained on the same dataset. Then, a second-level model, the meta-learner, is trained on the outputs of these base models. The meta-model learns how to best combine the predictions of the individual models to achieve improved overall performance.

Stacking is unique in that it allows for the integration of models that are based on different algorithms. This diversity can capture a broader range of patterns in the data and often leads to enhanced predictive power. The approach is particularly useful in competitions and complex real-world scenarios where maximizing performance is essential.

Real-World Applications

Ensemble learning has been adopted in many industries due to its effectiveness and versatility. Below are a few areas where ensemble methods have made a significant impact.

Fraud Detection

Fraud detection is a critical task in finance and e-commerce. Detecting fraudulent transactions involves analyzing vast amounts of data to identify patterns that indicate potential fraud. Ensemble learning techniques are well suited for this task because they can handle the inherent complexity and variability in transactional data.

By combining multiple models, ensemble systems can detect subtle signs of fraud that might be missed by a single model. For instance, one model might be effective at recognizing unusual spending patterns, while another may be better at identifying anomalies in transaction timing or location. When these models are integrated, the ensemble provides a more reliable detection system. Financial institutions use these advanced techniques to reduce losses and improve security.

Recommendation Systems

Recommendation systems are another area where ensemble learning shines. In industries such as e-commerce, streaming services, and digital advertising, personalized recommendations are key to engaging users and driving sales. Ensemble methods combine different recommendation algorithms to capture various aspects of user behavior.

Some models may focus on collaborative filtering, which relies on user interactions, while others may use content-based approaches that analyze item attributes. By integrating these methods, ensemble learning creates more comprehensive and accurate recommendation systems. This results in improved user satisfaction and increased conversion rates.

Healthcare and Medical Diagnosis

In healthcare, accurate predictions can have a profound impact on patient outcomes. Ensemble learning is used in medical diagnosis to combine insights from different diagnostic models. For example, in imaging diagnostics, an ensemble of models can be used to analyze medical images, each model focusing on different features of the image. The combined output leads to more reliable diagnoses, reducing the risk of errors.

Furthermore, ensemble methods help in predicting patient outcomes by integrating data from various sources such as electronic health records, laboratory tests, and imaging studies. The robustness of ensemble learning ensures that the predictions are reliable, even in the presence of noisy or incomplete data.

Marketing and Customer Analytics

Marketing campaigns increasingly rely on data-driven strategies. Ensemble learning techniques are applied to customer analytics to predict consumer behavior, segment audiences, and optimize campaign effectiveness. By combining multiple predictive models, companies can develop targeted marketing strategies that are more likely to succeed.

Ensemble methods help in identifying subtle trends in consumer data that may not be evident from a single model. The integration of different models enables marketers to refine their strategies continuously, ensuring that campaigns are responsive to changing consumer preferences and market conditions.

Industrial Applications

In manufacturing and other industrial settings, ensemble learning is used to predict maintenance needs, monitor quality, and optimize production processes. For example, sensor data from machinery can be analyzed using multiple models to predict failures before they occur. This proactive approach minimizes downtime and reduces costs, leading to improved operational efficiency.

The use of ensemble learning in industrial applications demonstrates its versatility. Whether it is monitoring complex systems or making real-time decisions, the integration of multiple models provides a robust solution that can adapt to diverse and challenging environments.

Challenges and Best Practices

While ensemble learning offers many benefits, it is not without its challenges. One of the primary challenges is ensuring that the individual models are sufficiently diverse. If the models are too similar, the ensemble may not perform much better than a single model. It is important to select or generate models that make different errors so that their combination results in a net improvement.

Another challenge is the increased computational complexity that often comes with ensemble methods. Training multiple models and combining their outputs can require significant processing power and memory. In many cases, this challenge is addressed through the use of cloud computing resources and optimized algorithms.

Interpretability is also a critical consideration. Ensemble models can be more difficult to interpret than simpler, single models. In applications where understanding the reasoning behind a prediction is important, such as in healthcare or finance, this lack of transparency can be a concern. To address this, researchers and practitioners often develop techniques to analyze and explain the behavior of ensemble systems.

Best practices for using ensemble learning in real-world applications include:

- Diversity in Model Selection: Ensure that the individual models are different in terms of structure and training data.

- Proper Validation: Use robust validation techniques to test the performance of the ensemble on unseen data.

- Scalability Considerations: Plan for the computational resources required, especially when working with large datasets.

- Interpretability Tools: Employ methods to explain how the ensemble makes its predictions, which can build trust among stakeholders.

- Continuous Improvement: Regularly update and retrain the models in the ensemble to adapt to new data and changing conditions.

Future Directions in Ensemble Learning

The field of ensemble learning continues to evolve as new techniques and technologies emerge. One promising area is the integration of deep learning models into ensemble systems. Deep neural networks have shown remarkable performance in various tasks, and combining them with other models can lead to even greater improvements.

Another direction is the development of more efficient algorithms that reduce the computational burden of ensemble methods. Researchers are actively exploring ways to streamline the training process and optimize the combination of models. This progress is likely to make ensemble learning more accessible to a wider range of applications.

There is also growing interest in hybrid ensemble methods that combine the strengths of different ensemble techniques. For instance, integrating bagging and boosting methods into a single framework may offer benefits that neither technique can achieve alone. These hybrid approaches hold promise for tackling complex problems that require a high degree of accuracy and robustness.

As machine learning applications expand into new domains, the need for reliable and interpretable models becomes even more critical. Ensemble learning is expected to play a key role in this evolution. With ongoing research and development, ensemble methods will likely become even more effective in solving real-world problems across industries.

Conclusion

Ensemble learning stands as a vital tool in the modern data scientist's toolkit. By combining multiple models, ensemble methods achieve improved accuracy, greater robustness, and enhanced generalization. This chapter has explored the principles behind ensemble learning, explained the key techniques of bagging, boosting, and stacking, and highlighted real-world applications in fraud detection, recommendation systems, healthcare, marketing, and industrial processes.

The practical benefits of ensemble learning are clear. In environments where data quality is variable and the stakes are high, ensemble methods provide a way to harness the strengths of diverse models. Although challenges such as computational complexity and interpretability remain, best practices and continuous research are paving the way for more efficient and transparent systems.

Looking ahead, ensemble learning is poised to drive further advancements in machine learning applications. Its ability to integrate various models into a coherent whole makes it an invaluable approach for tackling the complexities of real-world data. As technologies and techniques continue to evolve, ensemble learning will undoubtedly remain at the forefront of innovation in many industries.

In summary, ensemble learning is more than just a method for combining models. It represents a philosophy of collaboration among algorithms, one that leads to systems capable of tackling challenges that no single model could address on its own. The real-world success of ensemble methods in applications ranging from fraud detection to recommendation systems serves as a testament to their power and potential. With a solid understanding of ensemble techniques and best practices, practitioners can continue to push the boundaries of what is possible in machine learning.

CHAPTER 6

Random Forest in Real World

Random Forest is an advanced ensemble learning method that builds multiple decision trees to produce more accurate and robust predictions. This chapter provides an in-depth exploration of how Random Forest is applied in the real world. We will discuss the principles behind the method, explain its working mechanism in simple language, and provide detailed examples of its applications in medical diagnosis, stock market prediction, and cybersecurity. The chapter also examines the benefits and challenges of using Random Forest and considers its future potential in various industries.

Introduction

In today's data-driven world, decision-making processes rely heavily on machine learning methods that can interpret large volumes of data and provide actionable insights. Random Forest is one such technique that has gained significant popularity because of its ability to handle complex datasets and deliver reliable results. Its structure, which involves building numerous decision trees and combining their outcomes, offers a solution that is both flexible and resistant to overfitting.

The robustness of Random Forest makes it an excellent tool for applications where reliability is paramount. From predicting diseases in medical diagnosis to detecting anomalies in cybersecurity, the technique has proven its versatility. In the following sections, we delve into the core aspects of Random Forest and examine its use in real-world scenarios.

Fundamentals of Random Forest

Random Forest is based on the concept of ensemble learning, where multiple models are combined to achieve better performance than any single model could on its own. The method builds several decision trees during the training phase and merges their predictions to form a final output. This process helps reduce the variance in the predictions and increases the overall accuracy.

The primary idea is that while a single decision tree may be sensitive to noise in the data, a collection of trees can overcome these limitations by averaging out errors. This combination approach makes Random Forest a powerful tool for both classification and regression tasks. In classification tasks, the algorithm chooses the most frequent class among all the decision trees, whereas in regression tasks, it calculates the average prediction from all trees.

Another key concept in Random Forest is the idea of using random subsets of the data and random subsets of the features when building each tree. This randomness ensures that each decision tree is unique and that the overall model is less likely to overfit the data. The method is inherently robust against the challenges posed by high-dimensional data and correlated features, making it suitable for a wide range of applications.

How Random Forest Works in Practice

Data Sampling and Tree Building

When constructing a Random Forest model, the process begins with the selection of a random sample of the training data for each tree. This process, known as bootstrapping, involves drawing samples from the dataset with replacement. The outcome is that some instances may be repeated while others might be left out for that particular tree. Each tree in the forest is grown independently using these different subsets of data.

Once a bootstrap sample is selected, the model builds a decision tree. However, unlike traditional decision trees that consider all features when splitting a node, Random Forest randomly selects a subset of features. This additional layer of randomness ensures that the trees are diverse and that no single feature dominates the decision-making process across all trees.

Combining Predictions

After the trees have been built, the Random Forest model combines their predictions to form a final output. In classification tasks, this is typically done by taking a vote among all the trees. The class that receives the most votes is selected as the final prediction. In regression tasks, the model calculates the mean of the predictions from all the trees. This ensemble approach minimizes the impact of any single tree's error and produces a more stable and accurate prediction overall.

Real-World Implementation

In practical applications, the success of a Random Forest model depends on careful tuning of its parameters. The number of trees, the number of features to consider at each split, and the depth of each tree are all important factors that can affect the model's performance. Data scientists typically experiment with these parameters to find the optimal balance between accuracy and computational efficiency.

The method is implemented using widely available programming libraries in popular languages such as Python and R. These libraries offer built-in functions that make it easier to train, validate, and deploy Random Forest models. As a result, even practitioners with limited programming expertise can leverage this powerful technique in their projects.

Applications in Medical Diagnosis

One of the most impactful applications of Random Forest is in the field of medical diagnosis. Medical data is often complex and high-dimensional, which can present significant challenges for traditional analysis methods. Random Forest provides a way to sift through large amounts of data and identify patterns that can aid in diagnosing diseases accurately.

Early Disease Detection

In medical diagnosis, early detection of diseases such as cancer, diabetes, and cardiovascular conditions is critical. Random Forest models are capable of analyzing various patient indicators such as blood test results, imaging data, and genetic markers. By learning from historical patient records, these models can identify early warning signs and predict the likelihood of a disease developing in a patient. The ability to provide timely and accurate diagnoses can lead to more effective treatments and improved patient outcomes.

Reducing Diagnostic Errors

Medical errors can have severe consequences, and ensuring accurate diagnosis is a top priority in healthcare. Random Forest, with its ensemble approach, reduces the chances of misdiagnosis by relying on the collective wisdom of multiple decision trees. Each tree contributes to the final prediction, thereby reducing the risk that a single misleading factor will result in an incorrect diagnosis. This reliability is particularly valuable in situations where a misdiagnosis could lead to unnecessary treatments or delayed interventions.

Case Studies in Healthcare

Several hospitals and research institutions have implemented Random Forest models to support their diagnostic procedures. For example, studies have shown that Random Forest can effectively classify tumor types based on gene expression data. In other cases, the technique has been used to predict patient responses to specific treatments, helping clinicians to personalize therapy plans. These real-world implementations underscore the importance of Random Forest in modern healthcare and its potential to save lives.

Applications in Stock Market Prediction

The stock market is characterized by volatile and dynamic behavior that is influenced by countless variables. Predicting market trends is a challenging task that requires robust models capable of handling noisy and complex data. Random Forest has emerged as a popular method for stock market prediction because of its ability to process large datasets and identify meaningful patterns.

Analyzing Market Trends

Random Forest models are employed to analyze historical stock prices, trading volumes, and other market indicators. By learning from past data, these models can recognize patterns that may indicate future movements. Financial analysts use these insights to inform investment strategies and manage risks effectively. The ensemble nature of Random Forest ensures that the model remains resilient even when individual predictors are affected by market noise.

Managing Investment Risks

One of the most important aspects of stock market prediction is risk management. Investment decisions must be based on predictions that are as accurate as possible to minimize potential losses. Random Forest models, by averaging the outcomes of multiple decision trees, provide a more stable prediction that can help investors gauge market sentiment more reliably. The method also allows for the inclusion of a wide range of variables, from macroeconomic indicators to company-specific data, thereby offering a comprehensive view of the factors influencing stock performance.

Real-World Implementations

Financial institutions and hedge funds have adopted Random Forest models to enhance their trading strategies. These models are integrated into larger analytical systems that continuously monitor market conditions and adjust predictions in real time. The ability of Random Forest to handle complex, non-linear relationships in data makes it an indispensable tool in the highly competitive world of finance.

Applications in Cybersecurity

Cybersecurity is a field that is increasingly relying on advanced machine learning techniques to detect and prevent threats. The volume and variety of cyber threats are growing, making it difficult for traditional security measures to keep pace. Random Forest has become an effective solution for cybersecurity because of its ability to analyze large amounts of network data and identify unusual patterns.

Detecting Intrusions and Anomalies

Random Forest is particularly useful for intrusion detection systems. These systems are designed to monitor network traffic and identify suspicious behavior that may indicate a security breach. By analyzing a wide range of features such as connection frequency, data packet sizes, and access patterns, Random Forest models can distinguish between normal and anomalous network activity. This early detection of anomalies allows organizations to respond to threats before they escalate into serious incidents.

Enhancing Threat Intelligence

The cybersecurity landscape is constantly evolving, with new threats emerging regularly. Random Forest models can adapt to these changes by learning from new data, making them a dynamic tool in threat intelligence. They are used to classify different types of malware, detect phishing attempts, and monitor system logs for signs of compromise. The robust performance of Random Forest in these applications has made it a trusted component in many cybersecurity frameworks.

Real-World Success Stories

Many organizations have reported significant improvements in their security posture after implementing Random Forest-based solutions. For instance, several companies have successfully reduced the number of false positives in their intrusion detection systems, which in turn has allowed their security teams to focus on genuine threats. The ability of Random Forest to combine multiple indicators into a single, reliable prediction has proven invaluable in maintaining secure network environments.

Advantages and Challenges of Random Forest

Advantages

Random Forest offers several advantages that make it a popular choice in real-world applications. One of its main strengths is its robustness. By combining multiple decision trees, the method reduces the risk of overfitting and increases the overall stability of the predictions. Additionally, Random Forest is capable of handling large datasets and can work with a mixture of numerical and categorical features. Its ability to provide insights into feature importance is also valuable for understanding the factors that drive predictions in various applications.

Challenges

Despite its many advantages, Random Forest is not without challenges. One of the main drawbacks is the increased computational cost associated with building and maintaining multiple decision trees. This can be a significant concern when dealing with extremely large datasets or when real-time predictions are required. Another challenge is the interpretability of the model. While individual decision trees are relatively easy to understand, the ensemble nature of Random Forest can make it more difficult to explain how specific predictions are made. Addressing these challenges requires careful tuning of model parameters and sometimes the use of additional interpretability tools.

Future Perspectives

As data continues to grow in volume and complexity, the need for robust and reliable machine learning techniques will only increase. Random Forest is well positioned to remain a critical tool in the data scientist's toolkit due to its flexibility and performance. Researchers are continuously exploring ways to improve the efficiency of Random Forest, such as parallel processing and optimization of tree construction methods. Furthermore, the integration of Random Forest with other machine learning techniques may yield hybrid models that capitalize on the strengths of multiple approaches.

In fields such as healthcare, finance, and cybersecurity, the evolution of Random Forest models is expected to drive significant advancements. The ongoing research and practical implementations are likely to lead to models that are not only more accurate but also easier to interpret and faster to deploy. As a result, organizations will be better equipped to tackle complex challenges and leverage data in ways that were not possible before.

Conclusion

Random Forest stands out as a versatile and powerful machine learning technique that has proven its value in a variety of real-world applications. Its ensemble approach, which combines multiple decision trees, offers robustness and reliability that are critical in areas such as medical diagnosis, stock market prediction, and cybersecurity. The technique effectively reduces overfitting, handles high-dimensional data, and provides insights into the importance of different features.

While the method comes with challenges, particularly in terms of computational cost and interpretability, its advantages often outweigh these concerns. With ongoing advancements in computational power and algorithmic research, Random Forest is likely to become even more integral to data-driven decision making across industries.

As organizations continue to face the demands of an increasingly complex and dynamic environment, Random Forest will play a crucial role in enabling accurate predictions and informed decision making. This chapter has provided a comprehensive overview of how Random Forest operates in the real world, its applications, and the benefits it offers. The insights gained here lay the foundation for further exploration of ensemble learning methods and their impact on the future of machine learning.

In summary, Random Forest is not only a theoretical construct but also a practical tool that has demonstrated remarkable success in addressing real-world challenges. Its ability to combine the strengths of multiple decision trees into a single, cohesive model makes it an essential component in the toolkit of modern data science. As we move forward, the continued evolution and application of Random Forest will undoubtedly contribute to significant advancements in various fields, driving innovation and improving outcomes across multiple sectors.

CHAPTER 7

Dimensionality Reduction in Real World

Dimensionality reduction is a vital process for handling large and complex datasets in modern applications. In many fields, data is abundant and diverse. The high number of variables present in these datasets can lead to inefficiencies and challenges in analysis. This chapter explains how dimensionality reduction techniques such as Principal Component Analysis (PCA) and t-SNE help simplify the data without losing essential information. The discussion will focus on applications in image processing, natural language processing, and bioinformatics while highlighting practical insights and real world examples.

Introduction to Dimensionality Reduction

In today s digital world, many systems generate and collect vast amounts of data. This data is often represented in high dimensions. High-dimensional data can be challenging to analyze, visualize, and even store. Dimensionality reduction aims to convert data with many variables into a more manageable form. This process involves identifying and preserving the most important information while discarding noise and redundant features.

The need for dimensionality reduction arises in many real world scenarios. When working with images, each pixel represents a dimension. In text analysis, every word or phrase can contribute to the complexity of the data. In bioinformatics, large gene expression profiles produce a high number of features. Reducing dimensions in these cases helps improve computational efficiency, enhances visualization, and supports more accurate decision making.

The Importance of Simplification

High dimensional data can sometimes be overwhelming and difficult to process. When a dataset contains hundreds or even thousands of features, it becomes challenging for models to find meaningful patterns. In addition, many learning algorithms struggle with the curse of dimensionality. This term refers to various phenomena that arise when analyzing data in high dimensional spaces. By reducing the number of dimensions, it is possible to focus on the most significant patterns and trends.

Simplification is not only about reducing computational load; it also facilitates a deeper understanding of the data. A simpler dataset allows analysts and researchers to uncover hidden structures and relationships more easily. In real world applications, this simplification can lead to better predictions and more informed decisions. As a result, techniques for dimensionality reduction have become an essential part of the data scientist s toolkit.

Principal Component Analysis (PCA)

Principal Component Analysis is one of the most widely used methods for dimensionality reduction. The core idea behind PCA is to identify new axes, or directions, in which the data varies the most. These axes are known as principal components. Rather than working with the original variables, the data is reoriented along these components, which capture the most significant sources of variance.

PCA has several advantages in practical applications. First, it simplifies the data while retaining most of the important information. For instance, in image processing, PCA can reduce the number of features representing an image. This not only speeds up the processing time but also improves the performance of algorithms tasked with recognizing objects or patterns. In natural language processing, PCA can help manage large sets of word embeddings. By reducing the dimensionality of these embeddings, it is easier to visualize the relationships between words and phrases.

The technique is also used in bioinformatics, where it assists in analyzing complex gene expression data. High dimensional gene expression profiles can be transformed into a lower dimensional space, making it possible to identify patterns that correspond to different biological processes or diseases. With PCA, researchers can focus on the most important genes that contribute to variations in the data. This leads to more effective disease classification and a better understanding of genetic influences.

One of the key strengths of PCA is its ability to handle noisy data. In real world datasets, noise is almost always present. PCA works by highlighting the directions in which the signal is strongest and filtering out the less important variations. This leads to more robust models and clearer insights when interpreting the data.

t-SNE: A Technique for Visualization

Another powerful tool for dimensionality reduction is t-SNE, which stands for t-distributed Stochastic Neighbor Embedding. t-SNE is particularly useful for visualizing high dimensional data in two or three dimensions. While PCA focuses on maintaining the global structure of the data, t-SNE is excellent at preserving local similarities. In practice, this means that data points that are similar to each other in high dimensional space tend to be grouped together when the data is projected onto a lower dimensional space.

t-SNE is commonly used in fields that require a clear visual representation of complex data. In image processing, t-SNE can display clusters of similar images, making it easier for researchers to identify groups based on content. In natural language processing, t-SNE can illustrate the relationships between words, phrases, or even entire documents. For example, when applied to word embeddings, the technique reveals clusters that correspond to semantic similarities.

The benefits of t-SNE extend to bioinformatics as well. Researchers often use t-SNE to visualize high dimensional datasets such as single cell RNA sequencing data. By reducing the dimensions, t-SNE helps highlight distinct cell populations and their characteristics. This visual representation supports further analysis and leads to more accurate biological interpretations.

Despite its strengths, t-SNE is not without challenges. The technique can be computationally intensive and sensitive to parameter settings. It requires careful tuning to produce meaningful visualizations. However, when used properly, t-SNE offers an intuitive way to explore and understand high dimensional data in a manner that complements more analytical approaches like PCA.

Applications in Image Processing

Image processing is one area where dimensionality reduction techniques have a significant impact. Modern digital images consist of thousands of pixels, each contributing to the overall complexity of the image. When processing large sets of images, the high dimensionality can slow down algorithms and make pattern recognition more difficult.

PCA is often used to compress images. By representing the image in a lower dimensional space, the essential features are preserved while reducing the amount of data that needs to be processed. This makes it easier to perform tasks such as image classification and object detection. Additionally, t-SNE offers a means to visualize large image datasets. When images are mapped into a two dimensional space, clusters can emerge that reveal underlying patterns and similarities. This visualization supports the development of better image recognition models and improves our understanding of the data.

In practical terms, dimensionality reduction has enabled significant advancements in areas such as facial recognition, medical imaging, and remote sensing. By simplifying the data, researchers are able to train models more quickly and with higher accuracy. This leads to systems that can operate in real time and provide valuable insights across many domains.

Applications in Natural Language Processing

Natural language processing deals with the analysis and interpretation of human language. Text data is often unstructured and contains a large number of features. For example, when analyzing a document, each word can be considered a separate feature. Dimensionality reduction helps address this complexity by transforming the data into a more manageable form.

One common application of dimensionality reduction in natural language processing is the simplification of word embeddings. Word embeddings are representations of words in a high dimensional space. PCA can be applied to these embeddings to reduce their size while still preserving the semantic relationships between words. This makes it easier to perform tasks such as sentiment analysis, document classification, and machine translation.

t-SNE is also widely used in this field. When applied to word embeddings, t-SNE produces a visual map of the relationships between words. This map can reveal clusters of semantically similar words, offering insights into language structure and usage. Researchers use these visualizations to understand how language evolves and to identify trends in communication.

The ability to reduce dimensions without sacrificing important information is crucial in natural language processing. It not only enhances the performance of machine learning models but also enables researchers to better interpret and analyze large text corpora. With dimensionality reduction, the rich and complex nature of language becomes more accessible, supporting advancements in both academic research and commercial applications.

Applications in Bioinformatics

Bioinformatics is a field where the benefits of dimensionality reduction are particularly evident. Modern biological research generates large datasets that capture various aspects of living organisms. For example, genomic data may include thousands of measurements for each sample. Dimensionality reduction techniques help researchers make sense of this data by highlighting the most important features.

Principal Component Analysis is widely used in bioinformatics to analyze gene expression data. By reducing the number of dimensions, PCA allows researchers to focus on the key genes that influence biological processes. This simplification leads to more accurate classifications of disease states and a deeper understanding of the genetic factors at play. In many cases, dimensionality reduction has been essential in discovering biomarkers for diseases such as cancer and neurological disorders.

t-SNE is also gaining popularity in the field of bioinformatics. The technique is used to visualize high dimensional data, such as the results of single cell sequencing experiments. With t-SNE, researchers can observe distinct groups of cells and study their characteristics. This visualization is crucial for identifying cell types and understanding developmental processes. The ability to reduce and visualize dimensions has led to numerous breakthroughs in biological research and improved our understanding of complex systems.

Both PCA and t-SNE have their own strengths in bioinformatics. While PCA provides a robust way to reduce dimensions and highlight key variables, t-SNE offers a visual representation that can capture the subtle differences between individual cells or genetic profiles. Together, these techniques have transformed the analysis of biological data and continue to support cutting edge research.

Real World Challenges and Considerations

Although dimensionality reduction techniques offer many advantages, they are not without challenges in real world applications. One major challenge is the careful selection of parameters. The effectiveness of techniques such as t-SNE can depend on parameter settings that must be tuned to suit the specific data and application. Improper parameter selection can lead to misleading visualizations or loss of critical information.

Another challenge is maintaining the balance between simplicity and interpretability. Reducing dimensions too much can result in a loss of important details, while retaining too many dimensions may not yield the desired computational benefits. Finding the optimal level of simplification is essential for ensuring that the data remains useful and meaningful.

In addition, real world datasets often contain noise and inconsistencies. Dimensionality reduction techniques must be robust enough to handle these issues. While methods such as PCA are effective at filtering out noise, they may not completely eliminate all unwanted variations. It is important for practitioners to combine these techniques with other data preprocessing steps to achieve the best results.

Scalability is also a significant consideration. As datasets continue to grow in size and complexity, the computational requirements for dimensionality reduction can become substantial. Advances in hardware and algorithm optimization play a critical role in making these techniques practical for large scale applications.

Finally, it is essential to remember that dimensionality reduction is only one part of the data analysis process. It should be used in conjunction with other methods to fully explore and understand complex datasets. When applied thoughtfully, dimensionality reduction can serve as a powerful tool to uncover insights and drive innovation across many industries.

Conclusion and Future Directions

The use of dimensionality reduction techniques such as Principal Component Analysis and t-SNE has become indispensable in handling large and complex datasets. In image processing, these techniques allow for efficient storage and faster processing by simplifying image data without sacrificing important details. In natural language processing, they help to manage the vast number of features inherent in textual data and enable clear visualization of semantic relationships. In bioinformatics, they facilitate the analysis of high dimensional genetic data and support breakthroughs in understanding biological systems.

Looking ahead, the field of dimensionality reduction is likely to evolve with the integration of new methods and the development of hybrid approaches. As machine learning and artificial intelligence continue to advance, researchers are expected to combine traditional techniques with deep learning models to achieve even greater levels of performance and insight. The challenges of parameter tuning, noise management, and scalability will be addressed by ongoing research and improvements in computational infrastructure.

Dimensionality reduction remains a key component in the data analysis pipeline. It not only reduces computational burdens but also helps reveal underlying structures that are essential for understanding complex systems. As more data becomes available and the need for rapid analysis increases, these techniques will continue to play a central role in many fields.

In summary, dimensionality reduction transforms overwhelming data into clear, actionable insights. By focusing on the most important features, PCA and t-SNE enable more efficient analysis and open new avenues for research and innovation. The future of dimensionality reduction holds great promise, with ongoing advancements set to further enhance its applications in image processing, natural language processing, bioinformatics, and beyond.

CHAPTER 8

Unsupervised Learning in the Real World

Unsupervised learning is a powerful branch of machine learning that uncovers hidden patterns in data without the need for labeled examples. In this chapter, we explore the fundamental concepts of unsupervised learning and demonstrate its practical applications. The discussion covers key techniques such as clustering and association rule learning, and it examines how these methods are applied in market segmentation, anomaly detection, and customer behavior analysis. The following sections provide a comprehensive overview that spans theoretical foundations, real-world case studies, challenges, and future directions.

Introduction

In many real-world scenarios, data is available in large volumes without accompanying labels or classifications. In such cases, unsupervised learning provides valuable insights by discovering intrinsic structures and relationships in the data. Unlike supervised learning, which relies on predefined labels, unsupervised learning is entirely data-driven. Its ability to reveal previously unknown patterns makes it an essential tool for industries that rely on exploratory data analysis.

The significance of unsupervised learning has grown as the amount of raw data has increased exponentially. Businesses and researchers alike seek methods to extract meaning from unstructured data. Whether it is understanding consumer behavior, detecting unusual activity, or identifying emerging trends, unsupervised learning offers techniques that adapt to the complexity of modern datasets. This chapter focuses on how unsupervised learning is deployed in real-world applications and why it is critical for organizations seeking competitive advantages.

Understanding Unsupervised Learning

At its core, unsupervised learning deals with the organization of data by finding groups, patterns, or associations within it. This approach does not require any predefined labels, allowing the algorithm to determine the structure on its own. The primary goal is to model the underlying distribution or the inherent structure of the data.

One of the most compelling aspects of unsupervised learning is its flexibility. Since it does not rely on external input for guidance, the methods can be applied to a variety of data types. From text and images to transactional records and sensor data, unsupervised learning techniques work with nearly any dataset. This adaptability is particularly valuable in scenarios where human annotation is either impractical or impossible.

The process generally involves preparing a dataset, selecting an appropriate algorithm, and then letting the algorithm run to reveal clusters, associations, or other patterns. The results are often visualized using graphs or heat maps to help experts interpret the findings. In doing so, unsupervised learning transforms raw data into actionable insights without the need for constant supervision or intervention.

Key Techniques in Unsupervised Learning

Two of the most commonly used techniques in unsupervised learning are clustering and association rule learning. Each of these methods serves a distinct purpose and is suited for different types of data analysis.

Clustering

Clustering algorithms group data points based on similarity. The objective is to organize the data into clusters where members of each cluster share similar characteristics. Clustering is widely used in applications such as customer segmentation, image analysis, and document categorization. By analyzing clusters, businesses can identify groups of similar customers and tailor their marketing strategies to meet the specific needs of each segment.

Several popular clustering algorithms exist, each with its own set of strengths and limitations. Some algorithms excel at handling large datasets, while others perform better on data with complex distributions. The choice of algorithm often depends on the characteristics of the data and the specific goals of the analysis. In practice, clustering results can reveal hidden groupings that were not immediately apparent, making it easier for decision makers to understand the structure of their data.

Association Rule Learning

Association rule learning is another essential unsupervised learning technique. This method focuses on discovering interesting relationships between variables in large datasets. One common application is market basket analysis, where the goal is to identify products that are frequently purchased together. Such insights can be used to design targeted promotions and to improve store layouts.

The process involves analyzing transactions to find rules that indicate a strong association between items. For example, a rule might suggest that customers who buy one item are likely to purchase another. Retailers can use this information to create bundles or to recommend complementary products to shoppers. In addition, association rule learning is also applied in web usage mining, where the patterns of user navigation are analyzed to optimize website structure and enhance user experience.

Real-World Applications

The real-world impact of unsupervised learning can be observed across various industries. Below are some of the most common applications, each demonstrating the practical value of these techniques.

Market Segmentation

Market segmentation involves dividing a market into distinct groups of consumers with similar needs or preferences. Using clustering techniques, companies can analyze demographic, behavioral, and transactional data to identify segments within their customer base. This approach allows marketers to tailor their advertising strategies to the specific requirements of each group, thereby increasing the effectiveness of their campaigns.

For instance, a retail company might use clustering to determine that its customers fall into several distinct segments based on purchasing behavior. One segment might be comprised of frequent buyers of high-end products, while another may include budget-conscious shoppers. With this information, the company can design personalized marketing campaigns that speak directly to the interests and needs of each group, ultimately improving customer engagement and boosting sales.

Anomaly Detection

Another critical application of unsupervised learning is anomaly detection. In industries such as finance and cybersecurity, it is essential to identify unusual patterns that may indicate fraudulent activities or security breaches. Unsupervised learning algorithms are well suited for this task because they can flag outliers without prior knowledge of what constitutes normal behavior.

In financial institutions, for example, anomaly detection techniques are used to monitor transactions in real time. When a transaction deviates significantly from the norm, the system generates an alert for further investigation. Similarly, in cybersecurity, unsupervised learning helps detect abnormal network activity that may signal a potential intrusion. By continuously analyzing patterns in the data, organizations can maintain robust security protocols and respond swiftly to emerging threats.

Customer Behavior Analysis

Understanding customer behavior is vital for any business seeking to remain competitive. Unsupervised learning methods provide insights into how customers interact with products and services, enabling companies to refine their strategies and improve customer satisfaction. By examining patterns in customer data, businesses can identify trends, predict future behavior, and adjust their operations accordingly.

For example, a streaming service might use clustering to analyze viewing habits and recommend new content that aligns with each viewer's preferences. Similarly, e-commerce platforms can use association rule learning to determine which products are often viewed or purchased together. This analysis helps in designing personalized recommendation systems that enhance the overall customer experience and drive higher engagement levels.

Challenges and Considerations

While unsupervised learning offers many benefits, it also presents unique challenges that practitioners must address. One of the primary challenges is the lack of labeled data, which can make it difficult to evaluate the performance of the algorithms. Without a clear benchmark, it is often hard to determine whether the patterns discovered are truly meaningful.

Another significant challenge is the selection of the right algorithm and the appropriate tuning of its parameters. Unlike supervised learning, where performance metrics such as accuracy can guide the selection process, unsupervised learning relies on more subjective measures. Practitioners must experiment with different methods and validation techniques to ensure that the results are reliable and actionable.

Data quality is another concern in unsupervised learning. In many cases, raw data can be noisy or incomplete. It is essential to preprocess the data carefully to remove errors and to standardize formats. Failing to address data quality issues can lead to misleading results that hinder rather than help decision making.

Interpretability also poses a challenge. The patterns identified by unsupervised algorithms may not always be immediately understandable to non-experts. Visualization tools and descriptive statistics play an important role in translating the results into actionable insights. By presenting the data in an intuitive manner, organizations can bridge the gap between complex analysis and practical application.

Future Directions and Conclusion

The field of unsupervised learning continues to evolve rapidly, driven by advancements in computing power and the availability of vast amounts of data. Future research is expected to address current challenges such as algorithm selection, parameter tuning, and the integration of unsupervised methods with other machine learning paradigms.

One promising direction is the combination of unsupervised and supervised learning techniques. By leveraging the strengths of both approaches, hybrid models can provide more accurate and interpretable results. For instance, unsupervised learning can be used to pre-process data and to identify clusters, which can then be refined using supervised methods. Such hybrid systems have the potential to deliver superior performance in tasks ranging from fraud detection to personalized marketing.

Another area of interest is the application of unsupervised learning in emerging fields such as the Internet of Things and smart cities. As sensors and connected devices generate ever-increasing amounts of data, unsupervised learning will be critical in managing and interpreting this information. The ability to detect patterns and anomalies in real time will enable more efficient resource allocation, improved public safety, and enhanced overall quality of life.

In conclusion, unsupervised learning is an indispensable tool in the modern data landscape. Its ability to reveal hidden structures in unlabeled data makes it a versatile and powerful method for addressing complex real-world challenges. From market segmentation and anomaly detection to customer behavior analysis, the applications of unsupervised learning are both diverse and impactful.

As industries continue to adopt and integrate these techniques, the potential for innovation grows. The insights provided by unsupervised learning not only help organizations understand their current environment but also equip them to anticipate future trends. By overcoming challenges related to data quality, algorithm selection, and interpretability, practitioners can unlock new opportunities for growth and efficiency.

This chapter has outlined the core principles and techniques of unsupervised learning in the real world. It has also highlighted how businesses and researchers are leveraging these methods to gain a competitive edge. As you move forward in your exploration of machine learning, keep in mind that the journey of discovery in unsupervised learning is one of continuous adaptation and innovation. The future of data analysis is bright, and unsupervised learning will remain at the forefront of this exciting evolution.

CHAPTER 9

Artificial Neural Networks in the Real World

Artificial Neural Networks have become one of the most influential tools in modern technology. Inspired by the human brain, these networks are capable of processing complex patterns in data. They have a wide range of applications that touch many aspects of everyday life. In this chapter we explore the origins of neural networks, how they work, and the many ways they are used in the real world. We will discuss handwriting recognition, speech recognition, autonomous systems, and other significant applications. The discussion is intended to provide a deep understanding of the subject while remaining accessible to readers with a general background.

Introduction to Artificial Neural Networks

The concept behind Artificial Neural Networks comes from the attempt to mimic the way the human brain processes information. The human brain contains billions of neurons that work together to analyze and interpret a continuous stream of sensory data. Similarly, Artificial Neural Networks are composed of interconnected nodes or units that work collectively to learn from data. This design allows neural networks to identify patterns that are often too subtle or complex for traditional algorithms.

Neural networks are not built to simply repeat a set of rules. Instead, they learn from examples. During the training process, the network is exposed to large amounts of data. It then adjusts its internal settings until it can make accurate predictions or classifications on new data. This learning process is what makes neural networks so powerful and versatile. They have become a cornerstone of modern machine learning applications in a wide variety of fields.

The Architecture of Neural Networks

At the heart of every neural network is a collection of simple units that function together. These units, often called neurons, are arranged in layers. The first layer receives the raw data. Subsequent layers transform the data in ways that allow the network to recognize increasingly abstract features. The final layer produces the output. This layered structure is one of the key reasons neural networks are capable of handling complex tasks.

Each neuron in the network receives input from many other neurons. The connections between neurons carry weights that determine the influence one neuron has on another. During training, the network adjusts these weights based on the patterns it observes in the data. This adjustment is done iteratively so that the network gradually improves its ability to make correct predictions.

This process of learning is analogous to how a person might learn to recognize handwritten letters. Initially the person may not be able to distinguish between similar shapes. With practice and exposure to many examples, the person gradually becomes adept at recognizing even the most subtle differences. In a similar way, a neural network improves its performance through repeated exposure to data and continual adjustment of its internal parameters.

Handwriting Recognition

One of the most successful applications of Artificial Neural Networks is in handwriting recognition. This application has transformed the way postal services, banks, and other institutions process handwritten documents. The network is trained on thousands of examples of handwriting, each carefully labeled with the correct interpretation. Over time, the network learns to recognize various writing styles and subtle nuances in strokes.

Handwriting recognition systems help reduce the time needed to process documents and improve accuracy in data entry tasks. They have been integrated into systems that automate the reading of postal addresses and bank checks. The technology can differentiate between similar-looking characters and adapt to variations in handwriting that arise from differences in individual writing styles. This ability to learn from a diverse set of examples makes neural networks a natural choice for this task.

The benefits of handwriting recognition extend beyond postal and banking applications. Educational institutions use similar technology to grade handwritten assignments automatically. Mobile devices incorporate handwriting recognition to allow users to write notes naturally. In each case, the neural network works by analyzing the shapes and strokes of the characters and matching them to known patterns.

Speech Recognition

Speech recognition is another area where Artificial Neural Networks have made a significant impact. In speech recognition systems, the network is tasked with converting spoken language into written text. This process involves recognizing the sounds of speech and understanding the context in which words are used. Neural networks excel at this task because they are able to model the complex variations in human speech.

Modern speech recognition systems are built on networks that have been trained on vast amounts of audio data. They learn to distinguish between different voices, accents, and speech patterns. As a result, these systems have become highly accurate and are now used in a variety of applications. Virtual assistants, for example, rely on neural networks to understand and respond to voice commands. Similarly, transcription services use these systems to convert spoken content into text automatically.

One of the challenges in speech recognition is dealing with background noise and variations in pronunciation. Neural networks address these challenges by learning from a diverse set of audio recordings. Over time, the network improves its ability to filter out noise and focus on the relevant sounds. The result is a system that is both robust and adaptable, capable of operating effectively in a range of environments.

Autonomous Systems

Autonomous systems represent one of the most exciting frontiers in the application of Artificial Neural Networks. These systems include self-driving cars, drones, and robotics that operate with minimal human intervention. Neural networks are used to process input from multiple sensors such as cameras, radar, and lidar. They analyze the sensory data to identify obstacles, predict the behavior of other objects, and determine the best course of action.

In the context of self-driving cars, neural networks are used for tasks such as object detection and scene understanding. The network processes images from cameras and identifies pedestrians, vehicles, and traffic signs. It then makes decisions about braking, steering, and accelerating. This integration of perception and decision-making is essential for ensuring the safety and reliability of autonomous systems.

Drones also benefit from the use of neural networks. In applications ranging from aerial photography to search and rescue, neural networks help drones navigate through complex environments. The ability of neural networks to learn and adapt makes them ideal for applications where the environment may be unpredictable. By processing data in real time, the network can assist in avoiding obstacles and optimizing flight paths.

Robotics in manufacturing and service industries have similarly been transformed by neural network technologies. Robots are now capable of performing intricate tasks such as assembling delicate components or interacting with humans in customer service roles. In each case, the network provides the robot with the ability to interpret sensory data and execute precise movements. This capability is opening up new possibilities for automation in sectors that previously relied heavily on human labor.

Challenges and Future Directions

While the benefits of Artificial Neural Networks are clear, their application in the real world also presents a number of challenges. One significant issue is the quality of data. Neural networks require large amounts of high-quality data to perform well. In many cases, obtaining such data is a difficult and expensive process. Researchers are continually developing new techniques to augment existing data and improve the learning process.

Another challenge is the need for transparency and interpretability. In many applications the decision-making process of a neural network is not easily understood by humans. This can be problematic in scenarios where trust and accountability are paramount. Efforts are being made to develop methods that provide greater insight into how these networks operate. By doing so, developers hope to build systems that are not only accurate but also understandable to users.

Computational resources are another area of concern. Training large neural networks can require significant computing power and time. Advances in hardware and distributed computing are helping to address these issues, but there is still a need for more efficient algorithms. Future research is likely to focus on optimizing network architectures and reducing the computational demands of training.

Despite these challenges, the future of Artificial Neural Networks appears bright. As the technology continues to mature, we can expect to see an even greater integration of neural networks into everyday life. Researchers are exploring new architectures that mimic additional aspects of the human brain. Innovations in learning algorithms are making it possible for networks to learn from fewer examples and adapt more quickly to new tasks.

The potential of neural networks extends beyond current applications. In healthcare, for instance, neural networks are being used to analyze medical images and assist in early diagnosis. In finance, they are being employed to detect fraudulent activities and make predictions about market trends. In the realm of environmental science, neural networks help model climate patterns and predict natural disasters. Each new application reinforces the versatility and power of this technology.

Conclusion

In this chapter we have examined the role of Artificial Neural Networks in the real world. These networks, inspired by the human brain, have the ability to process complex patterns in data. They have been successfully applied in fields such as handwriting recognition, speech recognition, and autonomous systems. By learning from large amounts of data, neural networks continue to improve and expand their capabilities.

The journey of Artificial Neural Networks is ongoing. With every advancement the technology moves closer to replicating the extraordinary pattern recognition abilities of the human brain. The challenges that remain are significant but not insurmountable. Continued research and development promise to overcome these hurdles and further enhance the performance of neural networks.

As we look to the future, it is clear that Artificial Neural Networks will play an increasingly important role in our lives. Their ability to learn, adapt, and improve holds the potential to transform industries and create solutions to some of the most pressing problems of our time. Whether it is making our roads safer with autonomous vehicles or improving the efficiency of healthcare delivery, neural networks offer a pathway to a smarter and more connected world.

The exploration of neural networks in this chapter has provided insight into both the strengths and challenges of the technology. It is a reminder of how far we have come and how much potential remains. As we continue to integrate these systems into real-world applications, it is essential to balance innovation with a careful consideration of ethics, transparency, and efficiency. The future of Artificial Neural Networks is bright, and their continued evolution promises to bring about new opportunities and improvements across many fields.

CHAPTER 10

Deep Computer Vision in Real World

Deep computer vision has emerged as one of the most exciting and transformative fields in artificial intelligence. The advent of deep learning models such as convolutional neural networks has revolutionized the way machines interpret visual data. This chapter provides a comprehensive exploration of deep computer vision in real-world applications, covering the evolution of deep learning in image processing, its impact on industries, and the challenges faced when deploying these models outside the laboratory. The discussion focuses on practical applications including self-driving cars, medical imaging, and facial recognition.

Introduction to Deep Computer Vision

The development of deep learning has enabled significant progress in the analysis and understanding of images. Traditional computer vision relied on handcrafted features and rules that limited performance in complex scenarios. With the introduction of convolutional neural networks, computers gained the ability to learn hierarchical representations from raw pixels. These models automatically extract features at various levels of abstraction. Early layers might detect simple shapes and edges while deeper layers capture intricate patterns such as textures and objects.

This revolution in technology has not only boosted accuracy but also paved the way for real-time applications. Industries now deploy deep computer vision to perform tasks that were once considered too challenging for machines. From detecting pedestrians on busy streets to identifying early signs of disease in medical scans, the impact of deep learning is pervasive and continues to expand.

The Evolution of Deep Learning in Image Processing

Deep learning for computer vision began with the realization that neural networks could be trained on large datasets to overcome the limitations of manual feature extraction. Over the years, research and innovation have led to the development of robust architectures that are both efficient and effective. Early breakthroughs were marked by improved accuracy in image classification contests. These advancements demonstrated that models could not only match but exceed human performance in certain tasks.

The journey from simple networks to the complex architectures used today has been driven by increased computational power and the availability of large-scale labeled datasets. Researchers refined network designs to reduce overfitting and enhance generalization. The ability to transfer learning from one domain to another further accelerated progress. As a result, the deep learning community has built a vast array of models, each tailored to address specific challenges in computer vision.

Architecture and Techniques of Deep Vision Models

At the heart of deep computer vision are convolutional neural networks. These networks consist of multiple layers that process images through a series of operations. The convolutional layers scan the input image for features, pooling layers reduce the dimensionality to manage computational load, and fully connected layers interpret the features to produce predictions. The combination of these layers allows the network to learn complex representations without requiring explicit programming for each feature.

Training these networks involves feeding them large amounts of image data and iteratively adjusting the internal parameters. The process relies on optimization techniques that minimize the difference between the network output and the expected outcome. Researchers have introduced various techniques such as dropout and data augmentation to improve robustness and prevent overfitting. The resulting models are capable of handling diverse image recognition tasks with remarkable accuracy.

Self-Driving Cars: Navigating Through Complex Environments

One of the most widely publicized applications of deep computer vision is in the field of autonomous vehicles. Self-driving cars use cameras and sensors to interpret their surroundings in real time. The convolutional neural networks installed in these vehicles detect objects such as other vehicles, pedestrians, traffic signs, and road markings. By processing this visual information, the system makes decisions about speed, direction, and safety.

The integration of deep computer vision in autonomous systems has led to dramatic improvements in road safety. Advanced models can analyze complex traffic scenarios and predict the movement of nearby objects. This capability is critical in reducing accidents and enhancing the overall driving experience. Manufacturers invest heavily in improving these models to ensure that self-driving cars can operate reliably in varying weather conditions and unpredictable urban environments. The continuous evolution of these systems promises to further enhance the safety and efficiency of road travel.

Medical Imaging: Enhancing Diagnostic Capabilities

Deep learning has also made significant strides in the field of medical imaging. Medical professionals rely on high-quality images for diagnosis and treatment planning. Traditional image analysis required years of training and manual inspection, which sometimes led to delays or errors. Deep computer vision offers a solution by automatically analyzing medical scans such as X-rays, CT scans, and MRIs.

Convolutional neural networks have shown exceptional ability in detecting anomalies and patterns that might be missed by the human eye. For instance, these models can identify tumors, fractures, or other abnormalities with high precision. This technology supports doctors by providing a second opinion and reducing the likelihood of human error. The integration of deep computer vision into clinical workflows has the potential to improve patient outcomes, reduce diagnostic times, and lower healthcare costs. Furthermore, these advancements open up new opportunities for early disease detection and personalized treatment strategies.

Facial Recognition: From Security to Personalization

Facial recognition systems are among the most familiar applications of deep computer vision. These systems have evolved from basic pattern matching to sophisticated models that can operate in a variety of lighting and environmental conditions. The ability to accurately identify individuals from photographs and video feeds has broad applications ranging from security and law enforcement to personalized user experiences on consumer devices.

Modern facial recognition systems employ deep learning to extract unique features from facial images. They compare these features against large databases to determine identity. The accuracy of these systems has improved dramatically due to the use of large training datasets and refined network architectures. In security, facial recognition provides a means to enhance access control and monitor public spaces for potential threats. On the consumer side, devices use facial recognition for unlocking phones and tailoring content to individual users. Despite the benefits, these systems also raise important privacy and ethical questions that must be addressed.

Challenges and Ethical Considerations

While deep computer vision offers many exciting possibilities, its implementation in the real world is not without challenges. One major issue is the requirement for vast amounts of annotated data. Acquiring high-quality datasets can be expensive and time-consuming. Moreover, data collected in controlled environments may not always reflect the variability encountered in real-world scenarios.

Another challenge is the interpretability of deep learning models. Although these systems can achieve high levels of accuracy, their decision-making processes are often opaque. This lack of transparency can lead to difficulties in understanding and trusting the outcomes of these models. Efforts are underway to develop techniques that provide insight into the inner workings of neural networks without compromising performance.

Ethical considerations also play a significant role in the deployment of deep computer vision technologies. The use of facial recognition, for example, raises concerns about surveillance and privacy. There is a growing debate on the balance between technological advancement and the protection of individual rights. It is crucial that developers, policymakers, and the public engage in discussions to ensure that the technology is used responsibly and ethically.

Future Directions and Conclusion

The field of deep computer vision continues to evolve rapidly. Innovations in network architecture and training techniques promise to further enhance the capabilities of these systems. Researchers are exploring novel approaches that reduce the need for large amounts of labeled data and improve model interpretability. In addition, the integration of computer vision with other modalities such as natural language processing is opening up new avenues for multimodal learning.

As deep computer vision technology matures, its applications will expand across even more sectors. The potential benefits in healthcare, transportation, security, and beyond are immense. However, the journey from laboratory breakthroughs to real-world deployment requires careful consideration of technical, ethical, and societal factors. Collaboration among researchers, industry leaders, and regulators will be essential to ensure that the advancements in deep computer vision contribute positively to society.

In conclusion, deep computer vision stands as a testament to the power of deep learning. The transformative impact of convolutional neural networks has reshaped industries and created new opportunities for innovation. As we look to the future, the continuous improvement and responsible application of these models will be critical in addressing the challenges of tomorrow. The evolution of this technology promises a world where machines can see and understand the environment with ever-increasing accuracy, leading to safer roads, healthier populations, and more personalized experiences for all.

CHAPTER 11

RNNs and CNNs in the Real World

Recurrent Neural Networks (RNNs) and Convolutional Neural Networks (CNNs) have emerged as powerful tools in modern artificial intelligence. In this chapter, we explore how RNNs and CNNs are used in practical applications. We discuss the strengths of RNNs in processing sequential data and examine how CNNs excel in extracting features from visual information. We also study the combined approach that allows these models to address complex tasks such as video classification and real-time analytics.

Introduction

In recent years, artificial intelligence has experienced significant growth due to the advancements in deep learning. Two important architectures in this domain are RNNs and CNNs. RNNs are designed to handle sequential data. This ability makes them a natural choice for applications such as time series forecasting and speech recognition. On the other hand, CNNs are specialized for processing grid-like data structures, with images being the most common example.

As industries demand real-time decision making and analysis of large volumes of data, researchers have discovered that integrating RNNs and CNNs offers powerful solutions. Video classification, for instance, benefits from the combined strengths of these networks. By extracting spatial features using CNNs and then processing the temporal sequence with RNNs, it becomes possible to understand both the visual content and its evolution over time. This chapter provides a comprehensive overview of these technologies, emphasizing real-world applications and the challenges that accompany them.

Recurrent Neural Networks in Practice

Recurrent Neural Networks are a type of neural network that maintain an internal state to process sequences of data. Unlike feedforward networks that assume all inputs are independent, RNNs consider the context provided by previous inputs. This makes them particularly suited for tasks where the order of data points is significant.

Time Series Forecasting

One of the most important applications of RNNs is in time series forecasting. In many industries, forecasting future trends is critical for planning and decision making. For example, in finance, predicting stock prices or market trends can offer a competitive advantage. Similarly, in weather forecasting, analyzing sequential data from various sensors helps improve prediction accuracy.

Time series data is inherently sequential. Each data point is influenced by previous observations. RNNs can capture these dependencies effectively. By processing one element of the sequence at a time and updating their internal state, these networks develop an understanding of the underlying trends. This process results in forecasts that can adapt to changes and anomalies over time.

Speech Recognition

Another domain where RNNs have proven to be invaluable is speech recognition. Speech is a sequence of sounds that carry meaning. Recognizing words accurately requires an understanding of the context and the flow of speech. RNNs, with their memory capabilities, are able to maintain contextual information over time. This is particularly useful for recognizing spoken language in noisy environments or in cases where accents and speech patterns vary widely.

Modern speech recognition systems often incorporate RNNs to improve the accuracy of transcription. By processing audio signals in sequential order, these systems can predict the next sound or word based on prior context. The result is a more reliable and responsive tool for converting speech into text. This capability is essential for applications such as virtual assistants, transcription services, and automated customer support.

Convolutional Neural Networks and Their Role

Convolutional Neural Networks are specialized in handling data with a grid-like topology. They have become the backbone of many computer vision applications. The key strength of CNNs lies in their ability to automatically extract and learn features from images. They use layers that perform convolutions to detect edges, textures, and patterns that are fundamental for image understanding.

Visual Data Processing

CNNs are widely used in tasks such as image classification, object detection, and segmentation. In a typical scenario, an image is fed into the network, which then applies a series of convolutional layers to identify distinct visual features. This process enables the network to classify images based on the features it has learned. For instance, in a medical setting, CNNs can help identify anomalies in radiographic images, assisting healthcare professionals in diagnosing conditions accurately.

Feature Extraction in Videos

While CNNs excel in static image analysis, videos present additional challenges because they involve temporal changes. Each frame of a video is similar to a static image, but the sequence of frames carries important information about movement and transitions. CNNs can process each frame to extract spatial features, which then serve as input for further analysis. This role of CNNs is vital in scenarios where detailed analysis of visual content is required.

Combining RNNs and CNNs for Advanced Applications

The integration of RNNs and CNNs leads to a hybrid approach that leverages the strengths of both networks. This combination is especially effective in processing video data and enabling real-time analytics.

Video Classification

Video classification is a complex task that involves understanding both spatial and temporal features. CNNs are used to extract key features from each frame of a video. These features capture the visual details of the scene, such as objects, textures, and colors. Once the spatial features are extracted, RNNs take over to process the sequence of frames. The RNN interprets how these features change over time, allowing the system to classify the video based on both its visual content and the evolution of that content.

For example, in a security system, video classification can help distinguish between normal activities and suspicious behavior. The CNN processes the visual data to identify objects and scenes, while the RNN analyzes the sequence to detect unusual movements. This combined approach leads to more accurate detection and faster response times in real-world applications.

Real-time Analytics

Real-time analytics require systems that can process and analyze data as it is generated. In many modern applications, such as surveillance systems or live event monitoring, data is continuously streamed and must be interpreted instantly. By combining the feature extraction capabilities of CNNs with the sequence processing strengths of RNNs, systems can analyze video feeds in real time.

In such applications, the CNN operates on each frame to extract meaningful features quickly. The RNN then assesses the sequence of features, detecting patterns or anomalies that require immediate attention. This method is not limited to video data. It can be applied to other types of sequential information, such as sensor data in industrial automation or traffic data in smart city management. The result is an integrated system that delivers actionable insights with minimal delay.

Challenges and Best Practices

While the potential of RNNs and CNNs is significant, deploying these models in real-world environments comes with challenges. Addressing these issues is crucial for ensuring that the systems are both effective and reliable.

Data Quality and Preprocessing

High-quality data is essential for training both RNNs and CNNs. In real-world scenarios, data can be noisy, incomplete, or unbalanced. Careful preprocessing is required to clean and prepare the data for training. This process might include normalization, augmentation, and the removal of outliers. For video data, additional steps such as frame sampling and synchronization are often necessary to ensure that the sequential information is preserved.

Computational Requirements

Training deep learning models can be computationally intensive. Large datasets, particularly video data, demand significant processing power and memory. It is common to use specialized hardware such as graphics processing units (GPUs) or tensor processing units (TPUs) to accelerate training. Cloud-based solutions offer scalable resources that make it easier to manage the computational load. Efficient use of these resources is important to keep the training times reasonable and to deploy models that can operate in real time.

Integration and Deployment

The integration of RNNs and CNNs into a single system requires careful design. The handover between spatial feature extraction and temporal sequence processing must be seamless. It is essential to ensure that the output from the CNN is formatted correctly for input into the RNN. Developers often experiment with different architectures and layer configurations to optimize performance. Deployment in production also requires considerations such as latency, model size, and the ability to update the system as new data becomes available.

Ethical and Practical Considerations

As these models are applied to sensitive areas such as surveillance or healthcare, ethical considerations come into play. Ensuring data privacy and addressing bias in model predictions are critical steps. Transparency in how the models make decisions helps build trust among users and stakeholders. Continuous monitoring and updating of the systems are necessary to maintain performance and adapt to changing environments.

Future Directions

The field of deep learning continues to evolve rapidly. Researchers are constantly developing new techniques to improve the performance and efficiency of RNNs and CNNs. Future developments are likely to include more robust hybrid models that can handle even more complex data types. Innovations in hardware and software will drive the ability to process large datasets more quickly and accurately.

Emerging applications are also pushing the boundaries of what these models can achieve. For instance, advances in augmented reality and virtual reality rely on real-time analytics that combine spatial and temporal data processing. Autonomous systems, such as self-driving cars, require continuous interpretation of a dynamic environment. The combination of RNNs and CNNs is expected to play a key role in making these systems more reliable and responsive.

Furthermore, interdisciplinary research is exploring how these models can be integrated with other techniques such as reinforcement learning and unsupervised learning. The convergence of these approaches may lead to systems that not only analyze data but also learn and adapt from the outcomes of their decisions. This progress has the potential to create more intelligent and autonomous systems that can operate in complex real-world environments.

Conclusion

This chapter has provided an in-depth look at the role of RNNs and CNNs in real-world applications. RNNs, with their ability to process sequential data, are indispensable for tasks such as time series forecasting and speech recognition. CNNs, on the other hand, excel at extracting spatial features from images and video. The integration of these models opens up new possibilities, particularly in video classification and real-time analytics.

While the power of these models is evident, challenges related to data quality, computational requirements, and ethical considerations remain. Addressing these issues is key to unlocking the full potential of deep learning technologies. As research and technology continue to advance, the combined use of RNNs and CNNs is poised to play an even more prominent role in solving complex problems across diverse industries.

In the next chapters, we will explore additional architectures and techniques that complement the methods discussed here. The journey into deep learning is ongoing, and every advancement brings us closer to systems that understand and interact with the world in more meaningful ways.

CHAPTER 12

NLP in Real World

Natural Language Processing (NLP) is a powerful branch of artificial intelligence that allows machines to understand and generate human language. The rapid advancement of NLP technologies has revolutionized the way we interact with computers and each other. In this chapter we explore the fundamental concepts of NLP and its applications in real-world scenarios. We will examine how NLP drives innovations such as chatbots, sentiment analysis, and automatic translation while also addressing the challenges and ethical considerations that arise in its deployment.

Introduction: The Impact of NLP

The way people communicate has always been at the center of human progress. With the explosion of digital data and the increasing need for automated information processing, Natural Language Processing has emerged as a critical tool for understanding text and speech. From simplifying customer service operations to breaking down language barriers across the globe, NLP has a profound impact on everyday life. By converting unstructured data into actionable insights, NLP empowers businesses, governments, and individuals to make informed decisions and enhance user experiences.

The evolution of NLP has been driven by advancements in computing power, the availability of large datasets, and improvements in algorithm design. Today, NLP systems are capable of tasks that were once considered the exclusive domain of human experts. In the following sections we discuss the building blocks of NLP and explore how it is applied in various industries.

Foundations of Natural Language Processing

At its core, NLP is concerned with the interaction between computers and human language. The objective is to enable machines to comprehend the meaning behind words, sentences, and larger bodies of text. Early efforts in this field focused on rule-based approaches, where linguistic rules were manually encoded. Over time these methods evolved into statistical and data-driven techniques that leverage large corpora of text data.

Modern NLP systems employ a variety of methods to process language. They begin with text preprocessing steps that include tokenization, where text is broken into words or phrases, and normalization, which standardizes text by converting it into a uniform format. This preprocessing is followed by the extraction of linguistic features, which are used to build models capable of tasks such as classification and prediction.

Language models are central to NLP and come in many forms. Some systems rely on simpler models that estimate the likelihood of word sequences while others use complex deep learning architectures to capture nuanced meanings and context. Although the underlying techniques differ, the goal remains the same: to bridge the gap between human language and machine understanding.

NLP Applications in Chatbots

Chatbots are one of the most visible applications of NLP in the real world. These systems provide automated responses in customer service, technical support, and online sales. By processing natural language inputs, chatbots can offer personalized assistance and resolve queries quickly, reducing the need for human intervention.

How Chatbots Work

The operation of a chatbot involves several key components. First, the system receives user input in the form of text or speech. NLP algorithms then analyze this input to determine its intent and extract relevant information. Based on this understanding, the chatbot selects or generates an appropriate response. Many systems use predefined response templates combined with real-time data to deliver accurate and context-aware answers.

A crucial element in the design of chatbots is their ability to maintain a coherent dialogue over multiple interactions. This requires the system to track conversation context and adapt its responses as new information emerges. Recent advances in deep learning have enabled chatbots to better manage long conversations and provide more human-like interactions.

Real-World Examples

Numerous industries have embraced chatbots as a tool for enhancing customer engagement. In the retail sector, chatbots assist customers by recommending products and answering questions about order status. In the financial services industry, they provide support by guiding users through complex procedures such as loan applications and account management. Healthcare organizations use chatbots to offer preliminary medical advice and appointment scheduling, thereby easing the burden on medical staff.

The success of chatbots in real-world applications is largely due to their scalability and cost efficiency. By automating routine inquiries, businesses can allocate resources to more complex tasks and improve overall customer satisfaction.

NLP Applications in Sentiment Analysis

Sentiment analysis is another transformative application of NLP. It involves the process of determining the emotional tone behind a body of text. This technology is widely used to gauge public opinion, monitor brand reputation, and analyze customer feedback.

Understanding Sentiment Analysis

Sentiment analysis systems use a combination of linguistic techniques and statistical methods to classify text as positive, negative, or neutral. These systems work by identifying key phrases and expressions that indicate sentiment. For instance, words that convey strong emotions are flagged, and the overall context is used to determine the sentiment of a sentence or document.

A robust sentiment analysis system takes into account the nuances of language, including sarcasm and idiomatic expressions. The complexity of human emotions means that even the most sophisticated models can sometimes misinterpret sentiment. Nonetheless, continuous improvements in NLP algorithms are steadily increasing the accuracy of these systems.

Applications Across Industries

Businesses rely on sentiment analysis to monitor social media, customer reviews, and other online content. This insight allows companies to respond proactively to customer concerns and adjust their marketing strategies. For example, if a new product launch is met with negative sentiment on social media, a company can quickly investigate and address the underlying issues.

Political organizations and news outlets also use sentiment analysis to track public opinion on current events and policy decisions. This data can provide valuable insights into voter behavior and the overall impact of political campaigns. In the entertainment industry, sentiment analysis helps producers gauge audience reactions to movies, television shows, and music releases.

By analyzing vast amounts of text data in real time, sentiment analysis provides organizations with a pulse on public opinion that would be impossible to capture through traditional surveys and focus groups.

NLP Applications in Automatic Translation

Automatic translation is one of the most impactful applications of NLP. The ability to translate text between languages with speed and accuracy has opened up new possibilities for global communication and commerce. Automatic translation systems are widely used in travel, international business, and online content creation.

The Process of Translation

Translation systems first analyze the source text to understand its structure and meaning. This process involves breaking down sentences into their component parts and identifying the relationships between words. Once the meaning is understood, the system generates an equivalent sentence in the target language. Modern translation systems often use deep learning techniques that have been trained on millions of examples to produce natural and contextually appropriate translations.

The quality of translation has improved dramatically over recent years. While early systems produced stilted or literal translations, current models are capable of capturing idiomatic expressions and cultural nuances. Despite these advancements, challenges remain, particularly with languages that have less available training data or with texts that involve specialized vocabulary.

Global Impact

The benefits of automatic translation extend across many areas of society. For businesses, it enables the creation of multilingual content that can reach a broader audience. In education, translation tools make it easier for students to access academic materials in their native language. Governments and international organizations use automatic translation to facilitate diplomatic communication and support global initiatives.

Automatic translation also plays a vital role in breaking down language barriers in emergency situations. When timely communication is critical, reliable translation systems can help coordinate relief efforts and ensure that vital information is accessible to all.

Overcoming Challenges in NLP

While the applications of NLP are both numerous and exciting, there are significant challenges that must be addressed to fully realize its potential in real-world environments.

Data Quality and Language Diversity

One of the primary challenges in NLP is the quality of the data used to train models. Real-world text is often messy and unstructured, with slang, typos, and variations in language usage. In addition, many languages have fewer available resources than English, making it difficult to develop robust models for those languages. Ensuring data quality and expanding linguistic coverage are ongoing priorities for NLP researchers and practitioners.

Context and Ambiguity

Human language is inherently ambiguous and context-dependent. A single word or phrase can have multiple meanings depending on the situation. This ambiguity poses a significant challenge for NLP systems, which must use context to disambiguate meaning. Advances in contextual language models have improved the ability of systems to understand nuanced language, but there is still room for improvement, particularly in handling idiomatic and culturally specific expressions.

Ethical Considerations and Bias

NLP systems are only as good as the data they are trained on. If the underlying data contains biases, the resulting models can perpetuate those biases in their outputs. This can have serious consequences, especially in applications like sentiment analysis and automated decision-making. It is essential to continuously monitor and address these biases through rigorous testing and the inclusion of diverse datasets.

Ethical considerations also extend to privacy and security. As NLP systems process vast amounts of personal data, ensuring that this information is handled responsibly and securely is critical. Developers and organizations must adhere to strict data protection standards and be transparent about how data is used.

Future Directions in NLP

The field of NLP is evolving rapidly, with ongoing research promising to overcome current limitations and unlock new applications.

Advances in Deep Learning

Recent breakthroughs in deep learning have significantly advanced the capabilities of NLP systems. Techniques such as transformer models have revolutionized language understanding and generation. These models have already led to improvements in translation, summarization, and conversational AI. Future research will likely focus on making these models more efficient and accessible, paving the way for even broader adoption.

Integration with Multimodal Systems

One promising area of research involves the integration of NLP with other modalities such as vision and sound. By combining text analysis with image and audio processing, systems can achieve a more comprehensive understanding of the real world. For example, an application that integrates video analysis with speech recognition could provide real-time subtitles or assist in video indexing.

Personalization and Adaptability

As NLP systems become more advanced, there is a growing emphasis on personalization. Future applications may tailor language processing to individual users, taking into account personal preferences, context, and language style. This adaptability will enhance user experiences and make NLP tools even more effective in dynamic environments.

Addressing Global Needs

The future of NLP is also closely tied to making language technologies accessible to speakers of all languages. Researchers are increasingly focused on developing models that perform well in low-resource languages and dialects. These efforts will help ensure that the benefits of NLP are distributed globally and contribute to a more inclusive digital environment.

Conclusion

Natural Language Processing is at the forefront of a technological revolution that is transforming how we interact with the digital world. In this chapter we explored the core principles of NLP and examined its practical applications in chatbots, sentiment analysis, and automatic translation. We also discussed the challenges that arise from data quality, contextual ambiguity, and ethical concerns, and we looked ahead to exciting future directions in deep learning, multimodal integration, personalization, and global inclusivity.

As organizations continue to leverage NLP technologies, the impact on everyday life becomes ever more profound. Whether it is through enhancing customer service with chatbots, providing valuable insights through sentiment analysis, or breaking down language barriers with automatic translation, NLP is reshaping industries and opening new avenues for communication and understanding. The journey of NLP in the real world is ongoing and full of potential. By addressing current challenges and fostering innovative research, we can expect even greater breakthroughs that will further integrate natural language processing into the fabric of society.

The promise of NLP lies in its ability to make complex information accessible and useful. As we move forward the field will undoubtedly continue to evolve, offering smarter, more intuitive ways to interact with technology. This chapter serves as both an introduction and a roadmap for understanding how NLP is being applied today and how it may develop tomorrow. The future of human-computer interaction is bright, and NLP stands at the forefront of that future, bridging the gap between human expression and machine understanding.

CHAPTER 13

Reinforcement Learning in the Real World

Reinforcement learning is based on the idea that an agent can learn to make decisions by interacting with its environment. The agent performs actions and receives feedback in the form of rewards or penalties. Through repeated trials, the agent learns which actions yield the best outcomes. This method of learning mimics the way living creatures learn from experience, gradually improving their behavior over time.

The focus on trial and error means that reinforcement learning does not require pre-labeled data or explicit instructions for every possible scenario. Instead, the agent explores different strategies and learns which ones are successful. This adaptability is what makes reinforcement learning especially useful in dynamic and uncertain environments.

The ability of reinforcement learning to operate in complex environments has led to its adoption in various industries. Whether in robotics, where machines must adapt to physical surroundings, in gaming AI, where non-player characters must exhibit intelligent behavior, or in autonomous navigation, where vehicles must make split-second decisions, reinforcement learning offers a robust framework for continuous improvement and adaptation.

Basic Principles of Reinforcement Learning

At the heart of reinforcement learning are several fundamental concepts that govern how agents learn and evolve. These principles help structure the learning process and guide the agent toward optimal behavior.

The Agent and the Environment

In reinforcement learning, the agent is the learner or decision-maker, while the environment represents the external context in which the agent operates. The agent interacts with the environment by performing actions and receives feedback based on the outcomes of these actions. This interaction is cyclical, with the agent constantly updating its understanding of the environment based on new experiences.

Actions, States, and Rewards

Every decision made by the agent involves choosing an action that influences the state of the environment. States represent the current condition or situation of the environment, and actions are the choices available to the agent. After performing an action, the agent receives a reward that indicates the quality of the outcome. The goal is for the agent to learn a strategy that maximizes cumulative rewards over time.

Exploration and Exploitation

One of the key challenges in reinforcement learning is finding the right balance between exploration and exploitation. Exploration involves trying out new actions to discover their potential benefits, while exploitation focuses on using known actions that yield high rewards. Too much exploration may lead to inefficient learning, whereas too much exploitation can cause the agent to miss out on discovering better strategies. Finding the optimal balance is critical to the success of reinforcement learning algorithms.

Learning Through Feedback

Reinforcement learning is a continuous process where the agent refines its strategy based on feedback from the environment. As the agent gains experience, it learns to predict the outcomes of its actions and adjust its behavior accordingly. This learning process involves evaluating past actions and making incremental improvements over time. The feedback loop ensures that the agent becomes more proficient at achieving its goals as it accumulates more experience.

Reinforcement Learning in Robotics

Robotics is one of the fields where reinforcement learning has had a significant impact. Robots operating in real-world environments face numerous challenges, including dynamic obstacles, unpredictable conditions, and complex tasks. Reinforcement learning offers a way for robots to adapt to these challenges and learn how to perform tasks with increasing efficiency.

Learning to Interact with the Physical World

Robots often operate in environments that are difficult to fully model or predict. Through reinforcement learning, robots can learn to interact with their surroundings without relying on a complete understanding of every variable. For example, a robot might learn to navigate a cluttered room by continuously adjusting its movements based on sensor feedback. Over time, the robot develops an intuition for avoiding obstacles and finding the best path through a complex space.

Improving Manipulation and Dexterity

In addition to navigation, reinforcement learning is used to enhance a robot's ability to manipulate objects. Whether in industrial settings or household environments, the ability to grasp, move, and manipulate objects accurately is crucial. Robots learn how to handle different objects by experimenting with various grip strengths and movements. The trial and error process allows the robot to refine its actions and develop precise control, making it more adept at performing tasks such as assembling components or sorting items.

Real-World Applications

Several real-world applications highlight the potential of reinforcement learning in robotics. In manufacturing, robots equipped with reinforcement learning algorithms can adapt to changes on the assembly line, ensuring that production continues smoothly even when unexpected variations occur. In healthcare, robotic assistants are being developed to support medical professionals by learning how to handle delicate instruments and navigate complex operating rooms. These advancements are paving the way for robots that can work safely alongside humans in a variety of settings.

Reinforcement Learning in Gaming AI

Gaming has long served as a testing ground for artificial intelligence, and reinforcement learning has contributed greatly to the development of more intelligent and adaptive game agents. The ability of reinforcement learning agents to learn from experience makes them well suited for creating challenging and engaging gaming environments.

Creating Dynamic and Adaptive Opponents

One of the primary goals in game design is to create opponents that challenge players and adapt to their strategies. Traditional game AI often relies on fixed algorithms that can be exploited by experienced players. In contrast, reinforcement learning enables game agents to learn from their encounters with human players and modify their behavior over time. This leads to opponents that are less predictable and more engaging, enhancing the overall gaming experience.

Learning Complex Game Strategies

Many modern games involve complex environments and intricate strategies that require more than simple rule-based decision-making. Reinforcement learning agents have been shown to master sophisticated strategies in games ranging from board games to real-time strategy titles. These agents explore a wide range of tactics during the learning process and gradually converge on effective strategies that challenge even the most skilled human opponents.

Enhancing Player Experience

The incorporation of reinforcement learning into gaming AI can lead to more immersive and personalized experiences for players. By observing player behavior and adapting in real time, game agents can tailor their responses to match the style and skill level of individual players. This dynamic adaptation not only increases the challenge but also keeps the game fresh and exciting, as the AI continually evolves to provide a new and engaging experience.

Notable Achievements

Over the past few years, several high-profile successes in gaming AI have been achieved using reinforcement learning techniques. Game agents have demonstrated the ability to learn and excel in complex games that were once thought to be beyond the reach of artificial intelligence. These achievements have spurred further research and development, and the techniques developed in gaming are finding applications in other areas that require adaptive decision-making.

Reinforcement Learning in Autonomous Navigation

Autonomous navigation represents another area where reinforcement learning plays a crucial role. From self-driving cars to unmanned aerial vehicles, the ability to navigate safely and efficiently in real-world environments is a significant challenge. Reinforcement learning provides a framework for developing systems that can learn to make decisions in complex and ever-changing scenarios.

Navigating Complex Environments

Autonomous systems must contend with a wide variety of challenges when navigating real-world environments. These include dynamic obstacles such as pedestrians and other vehicles, varying weather conditions, and unpredictable road conditions. Reinforcement learning allows autonomous agents to learn from direct interaction with the environment, making adjustments based on real-time feedback. Through continuous learning, these agents develop the ability to respond to unforeseen circumstances, ensuring safe and efficient navigation.

Enhancing Safety and Reliability

Safety is a primary concern in autonomous navigation. Reinforcement learning contributes to this goal by enabling systems to learn optimal behaviors that minimize risk. By repeatedly testing different strategies in simulated environments and real-world scenarios, autonomous systems can identify the safest and most effective paths. This process of learning from experience helps in building robust systems that can handle the inherent uncertainties of real-world navigation.

Integration with Sensor Technologies

The success of reinforcement learning in autonomous navigation is closely linked to advances in sensor technologies. Modern autonomous systems are equipped with a range of sensors that provide detailed information about the surrounding environment. Reinforcement learning algorithms use this sensory data to build a comprehensive understanding of the environment and make informed decisions. The integration of sensor data with reinforcement learning techniques leads to systems that are both responsive and adaptive, capable of navigating complex landscapes with a high degree of precision.

Real-World Deployments

Several companies and research institutions are actively developing reinforcement learning-based autonomous navigation systems. These systems are being tested in urban environments, on highways, and in specialized settings such as warehouses and industrial sites. The practical experience gained from these deployments is invaluable, as it helps to refine the algorithms and improve overall performance. As reinforcement learning continues to evolve, it is expected to play an increasingly central role in the future of autonomous navigation.

Challenges and Opportunities

Despite its many successes, reinforcement learning faces several challenges when applied to real-world problems. Addressing these challenges is essential for unlocking the full potential of reinforcement learning and expanding its applications.

Sample Efficiency and Data Requirements

One of the primary challenges in reinforcement learning is the need for large amounts of data. Because the agent learns from experience, it may require many interactions with the environment before it can develop an effective strategy. This need for extensive sampling can be a hindrance, especially in environments where interactions are costly or risky. Researchers are exploring methods to improve sample efficiency, such as using simulations or leveraging prior knowledge, to reduce the amount of data required for effective learning.

Balancing Exploration and Exploitation

As previously discussed, finding the right balance between exploration and exploitation is critical to the success of reinforcement learning algorithms. Too much exploration can lead to inefficiency, while excessive exploitation may cause the agent to settle on a suboptimal strategy. Designing mechanisms that dynamically adjust this balance remains an area of active research and is essential for developing reinforcement learning systems that are both robust and adaptive.

Robustness and Generalization

In the real world, environments are complex and often unpredictable. Reinforcement learning agents must be capable of handling a wide range of scenarios without overfitting to a particular set of conditions. Achieving robustness and generalization is a challenge that researchers continue to address. Advances in training techniques, regularization methods, and simulation environments are helping to create agents that perform reliably across diverse settings.

Ethical Considerations

As reinforcement learning systems become more integrated into critical applications such as autonomous navigation and robotics, ethical considerations become increasingly important. The decisions made by these systems can have significant consequences for safety and fairness. It is essential to ensure that reinforcement learning models are designed with ethical principles in mind, that they are transparent, and that accountability is maintained throughout their deployment.

Opportunities for Innovation

The challenges faced by reinforcement learning also present opportunities for innovation. The ongoing development of new algorithms, better simulation environments, and improved sensor integration all contribute to the advancement of the field. Reinforcement learning has the potential to revolutionize industries by providing systems that learn and adapt in ways that were previously unimaginable. Continued research in this area promises to lead to breakthroughs that can address some of the most complex challenges in artificial intelligence.

Future Directions and Conclusion

The future of reinforcement learning in real-world applications is bright and full of potential. As research continues and more sophisticated techniques are developed, the capabilities of reinforcement learning agents will continue to expand. The integration of reinforcement learning with other areas of artificial intelligence, such as computer vision and natural language processing, is likely to lead to systems that are even more intelligent and adaptive.

Future research efforts will focus on improving sample efficiency and developing methods that allow agents to learn effectively from limited interactions. In addition, advances in hardware and sensor technologies will further enhance the ability of reinforcement learning systems to operate in complex environments. The potential for combining reinforcement learning with unsupervised and supervised learning techniques may lead to hybrid systems that can leverage the strengths of multiple approaches.

Reinforcement learning is already having a profound impact in areas such as robotics, gaming AI, and autonomous navigation. As the technology matures, its influence is expected to expand into new domains, driving innovation and transforming industries. The continued evolution of reinforcement learning promises to create systems that are not only more efficient and capable but also more aligned with the ethical and safety requirements of real-world applications.

In conclusion, reinforcement learning offers a framework for creating intelligent agents that learn through experience and adapt to complex environments. Its application in robotics, gaming, and autonomous navigation demonstrates the versatility and power of this approach. While challenges remain, the opportunities for innovation are vast, and the future of reinforcement learning is filled with promise. As we look ahead, the lessons learned from current deployments will guide the development of more advanced and reliable systems that can tackle the intricate problems of tomorrow.

The journey of reinforcement learning in the real world is one of continuous learning and adaptation. The systems developed today are laying the groundwork for future advancements that will further blur the lines between artificial intelligence and human-like learning. With each trial and error, reinforcement learning agents become more refined, more capable, and more integral to the technological landscape of our society.

Ultimately, reinforcement learning is not just a method for solving problems; it is a new way of thinking about how machines can learn from their environment and improve over time. This chapter has provided an in-depth look at the principles, applications, challenges, and future directions of reinforcement learning in real-world settings. As we move forward, the ongoing research and development in this field will continue to transform industries and redefine what is possible with artificial intelligence.

Congratulations! By reaching this point, you have developed a strong foundation in real-world machine learning applications. You have explored supervised, unsupervised, and reinforcement learning, learned about classification, deep learning, computer vision, NLP, and even worked with practical coding examples.

Now, you are equipped to take your machine learning journey to the next level. With this foundational knowledge, you can confidently explore advanced books and research papers. You can start using popular ML frameworks such as Scikit-learn, TensorFlow, and Keras to build and deploy your own machine learning models.

The world of AI and ML is vast and ever-evolving. Keep learning, experimenting, and applying these concepts in real-world scenarios. Whether you're working on software engineering projects, developing intelligent applications, or contributing to AI research, you are now ready to make an impact in the field of machine learning.

Happy learning and coding!